Clubhouse Stories

Anna Jean

Text copyright © Anna Jean 1999

The author asserts the moral right
to be identified as the author of this work

Published by
The Bible Reading Fellowship
Peter's Way, Sandy Lane West
Oxford OX4 5HG
ISBN 1 84101 022 7

First published 1999
10 9 8 7 6 5 4 3 2 1 0

All rights reserved

Acknowledgments
Scripture quotations are from the Contemporary English Version ©
American Bible Society 1991, 1992, 1995. Anglicizations © British and
Foreign Bible Society 1997.

A catalogue record for this book
is available from the British Library

Printed and bound in Great Britain by
Caledonian Book Manufacturing International, Glasgow

Clubhouse Stories

Contents

Introduction	7
Lost!	9
A.S.L.T.W.	37
Bare cupboards	61
Help, I'm falling!	85
Sample drama script	111

With heaps of thanks to Ruth and Rebecca Haggis, Harrison Tatem-Wyatt, and Rebecca Percy, who were my young advisers on the text, and to Matthew Kent, Tony Start, Dawn Pacey and Erica Okure, who became my live Clubhouse gang, together with Katie Blockley, Anu Shajpal, Helen Morley, Karen Kortez, Jason Barry and Carrie Wright, who played the other characters in 'Lost!' Also to the rest of my family and friends who put up with not seeing much of me while I was writing this!

Introduction

Welcome to the world of the Clubhouse Stories!

The idea for *Clubhouse Stories* came about because I was curious to know more about the people Jesus talked about in his parables. The parables are, of course, stories that Jesus told to explain things about God in ways that the people of his day could understand. But the stories were always too short for me! So I started to think about what else might have happened to the people in Jesus' stories. I began to give them names, and imagined who else might have been involved in their lives.

And then I began to think about stories that would tell a modern version of some of the parables. After all, not many of us keep flocks of sheep, or know any pearl sellers, meet too many Pharisees, or own a vineyard! As I thought about the parable of the shepherd who doesn't rest until he's found his lost sheep, the idea of a lost cockroach as a parallel story just popped into my head, and wouldn't go away! Maybe you think I should have chosen something nice, like a dog or a cat, but I'm sure someone, somewhere, must like cockroaches. Paul, in my story, certainly does, which is why he's so keen to find the one he loses!

Each story is told bit by bit, so you'll have a part of the Clubhouse gang's story, followed by a parallel part of the parable, and so on. I'm sure you'll quickly get the idea! The book is intended to provide stories to read and enjoy, but it can also be used to create your own drama sketches for school assemblies and Sunday clubs, so that others can understand the parables, too. I created a script of the first story for my children's school's 'Need to Read' project, when 'Lost!' was narrated and acted out. Paul describes at the end of the book how you might do the same sort of thing.

Please do remember, though, that the expanded version of the parables in my book comes out of my own imagination. You'll need to check out the Bible version to see exactly what Jesus said (and every story contains a Bible reference, if you look carefully).

I hope you enjoy both the children's stories and the parables, and through them get to know something more about what Jesus wanted to tell us about God.

'Eight-fifty—rats! I'm late!'

Paul's watch was too expensive ever to be wrong. He leapt off the wooden platform into mid-air, grabbed the rope dangling in front of him, and slid down to the ground at breakneck speed. No time for using the ladder! Even so, he ran part of the way up to his house backwards, so he could admire the treehouse from a distance.

His dad said he'd get something built in their oak tree, but even Paul hadn't expected anything quite this good! Now at last the four of them had their own private Clubhouse. No more having to be quiet round at Nathan's in case they disturbed his gran; no more having to put up with Sam's four older brothers muscling in on things at her place, and definitely no more having to listen to Jessie's mum's singing!

He raced through the sun-lounge, slicking down his thick, fair hair as he went, and grabbed his school things from the bottom of the stairs. He yelled a hasty goodbye to his mum, who was just on the point of leaving for work herself (something high-powered in an office, though he could never remember what), stopped for a second to admire a huge, white Pyrenean mountain dog just entering his dad's vet's surgery, attached to the side of their house, and scooted off down the road in the direction of Fairview Secondary.

As he skidded through the school gate, Nathan and Sam, along with several others similarly dressed in red and grey, were already making their way towards the main entrance. Nathan—as short, skinny and perpetually scruffy as Paul was tall, slim and smart—was shuffling along miserably, his badly cut brown hair flopping into his eyes, while Sam (short for Samantha, a name which didn't suit her sporty, boyish image one little bit, and to which she mostly refused to answer!) was doing her best to cheer him up. Paul ran to join them, leaping on to the step in front of them, grinning broadly and stopping them in their tracks.

'Hiya!' Sam put up a hand and Paul brought his against hers to make a satisfyingly sharp slap. 'Good job someone's cheerful today!'

'That's because the Clubhouse is finished!' Paul announced triumphantly. 'You've just got to see it! None of your rough and ready stuff. Dad's carpenter's made it strong enough to survive a tornado!'

'Don't have tornadoes in England,' Nathan muttered.

'Do so! There was a tornado on the Isle of Wight a year or so ago. Don't you remember?' He punched him lightly on the arm, but Nathan just walked on into school. 'What's up with him today?' he asked, frowning at Sam.

'His mum's lost her job, his gran's lost her teeth, and his sister refuses to lose herself!' Sam grinned, then wrinkled up her nose. 'Oh, yes, and his dad's working abroad again—for six months—so it'll be Christmas before he sees him. Apart from that, he's fine!'

'Oh, well,' Paul waved his hand as though he could simply brush away Nathan's troubles. 'He'll feel better when he's seen the Clubhouse.'

They caught Nathan up in their classroom. He and Paul sat next to each other, near the back, and Sam and Jessie—the youngest in the gang, and whose parents came from Jamaica—sat directly in front. So far, there was no sign of Jessie.

As they sorted out books for the first lesson, Paul continued enthusiastically. 'The treehouse is really big, with wooden seating all round the walls, and square look-out points at different levels, with shutters on the inside to keep the rain out, and a platform bit at the front with a wooden ladder—oh, and a rope for quick escapes!'

'Sounds brilliant—eh, Nathan?' grinned Sam. 'We'll come and inspect after school today.'

'Maybe,' he shrugged, 'but Jessie won't be able to. I went round to see her last night and she's still not well. My mum wasn't very pleased—about me going, I mean. She worries I'll take germs back to Gran. But,' he sighed, 'she's my friend, I told her, and we have to cheer her up, don't we?'

Sam giggled at the thought of Nathan managing to cheer anyone up in his present mood, then tried to hide it with a cough. They'd been friends since Nursery, and she knew life at home wasn't easy with his dad away.

'I'll go and see her tonight,' Paul said. 'After I've shown you both the Clubhouse.'

Nathan shook his head. 'Expect it'll rain anyway.'

'Won't matter! The roof's covered with two layers of tarpaulin!' Nathan still looked gloomy. 'I know! Help me feed my cockroaches at lunch break. That'll make you feel better!'

'Yuk!' was Nathan's only response. Paul had brought a collection of cockroaches into the school lab a couple of weeks earlier and seemed to think they were great. He was the only one who did!

'They're not "yuk"—they're stupendous! I've hatched out seven species. Some of them can fly, though most don't, and they don't shed just one skin, like most insects, they shed loads!'

'So glad somebody loves them!' teased Sam. 'We'd absolutely adore to hear more but fortunately it's time for assembly!'

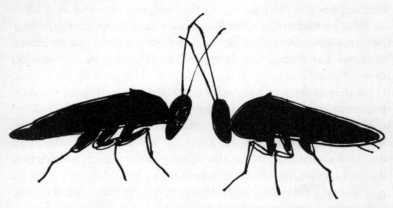

Nathan wasn't anywhere to be seen after lunch, so Paul went alone to the lab. He'd vaguely remembered being asked by Miss Grant, their form teacher, to help in the library, as the weather had turned bad and everyone was allowed to stay in, but wasn't Mr Deakin, their Science teacher, always going on about 'getting one's priorities right'? 'And, let's face it,' he thought, 'looking after my cockroaches is far more important than checking up on who borrows what books!'

The lab was empty. Great! At the back on a tall metal trolley stood a large tank, skilfully divided up into sections to keep the different species of cockroach separate (his dad's carpenter again!) Paul lifted the catches on the lid, and gazed at the insects in great admiration. What had started out as a simple school project had now become an all-consuming fascination!

'Did you know,' he'd told Sam, 'that cockroaches are one of the oldest types of winged insects in the world, dating back more than 350 million years! Cool, or what?!'

And though he wasn't sure if he believed in God most of the time, when he looked at these creatures he couldn't help admitting that whoever had made them had done a pretty brilliant job! They'd hatched out of small white eggs and grown quickly into mature insects, with two sets of wings, incredibly long antennae and a surprising variety of colourings and sizes. In fact, they were nothing short of amazing! So far, though, he'd not been too successful in convincing anyone else of this!

Paul pulled a bag of apple pieces out of his pocket, dropped bits into each section, then began counting the insects. He counted them every day, so knew perfectly well that, right now, there were twenty-five, but he liked to keep a check. He'd given them all names (like Hercules, one of the dark-brown 45-mm American species; Micro, an 8-mm speckled 'Lesser'; or Helmut, a pale, thin German type). He hadn't told anyone he'd given them names. They thought he was daft enough just liking cockroaches! Counting them also gave him an excuse to let some of them crawl up his sleeve, which he particularly liked doing. The way they moved fascinated him.

Suddenly Miss Grant entered the lab. 'Paul, here you are! You promised to help in the library this lunch break. Surely you haven't forgotten?'

'Er—no, Miss Grant.' Paul quickly brushed the cockroaches off his arm and closed the lid. 'I was just checking up on my—on these.'

The teacher glanced across at the tank and visibly shivered. Horrid things! 'Well, you're not supposed to be!' She opened the lab door. 'Quickly, now.'

'Yes, Miss Grant.' Paul did his best to stifle a groan. He knew where he'd prefer to spend his lunch break, and it certainly wasn't in the library! But, a promise was a promise, so he hurriedly secured the lid of the tank, and reluctantly followed her out of the lab, looking back over his shoulder regretfully as he closed the door.

About 2,000 years earlier, on a sun-baked hillside overlooking Nazareth in Israel, Joshua (grey-bearded and lean, with a face that looked like it was made of folded leather) was looking after his one hundred sheep. He knew there were one hundred, because he counted them every day—sometimes more than once a day—and that wasn't just to pass the time, either! He'd been looking after sheep and goats since he was twelve, and knew only too well how many wild creatures up on those hills considered sheep, in particular, a very tasty meal indeed! A shepherd had to be constantly on his guard in order to keep his flock safe.

'You must look out for lions, leopards, bears, wolves, hyenas, jackals, snakes and scorpions,' his father had instructed him (more years ago than Joshua cared to remember), listing them off on his fingers and making his son repeat them carefully. 'And don't forget the most dangerous animals of all,' he'd added with a grimace, '… the ones on two legs! Thieves will steal your whole flock, given half a chance. So count your sheep! Always know where each one is.'

'What happens if I lose one?' young Joshua had asked, eyes wide with apprehension.

'Then I must pay our master for it. And if one is attacked, we have to take back evidence to prove it.'

Joshua had nodded gravely and, in private, had 'practised' bravely fighting off everything on four legs, two legs, and no legs at all, until the day inevitably came when he'd had to do it for real, which, though more scary, had been a lot more exciting! And although at first he'd most feared the biggest animals, he soon decided snakes and scorpions were actually the worst, because you almost never saw them coming until it was too late.

Forty years later, and now with his own flock on those same hills, he still counted. But now he did it because, actually, he was pretty fond of his sheep. What had once been a job that simply had to be done so that he and his family could survive had turned, over the years, into a recognition that it was his sheep that were keeping him alive. Caring for them and keeping them safe was what made him want to climb that hill each morning and live just one more day. And, each day, just one day more.

His sheep had, in short, become his friends. And they were all quite amazingly different, in spite of what his wife said.

'You can't possibly tell one from another,' Miriam had often stated dismissively, peering into the large pen beside their home where Joshua kept them when they weren't grazing up on the hills. 'A sheep is a sheep, is a sheep!'

But she was wrong! He'd seen these animals being born; had seen each one take its first wobbly steps as a spindly little lamb; had looked after them lovingly as they'd grown, and knew each one as though they were his own children. He knew which ones were nervous so needed special care, and which were too brave for their own good! There was Bathsheba: if a sheep could be said to be beautiful, it was that one! And Delilah: a troublemaker from the moment she was born! And Deborah, who always took the lead, especially when there was any danger to be avoided. Naming each one had happily occupied several solitary hours up on those hills. He'd never admitted to Miriam that he had names for them all, of course. She thought he was daft enough as it was!

On this particular day, he'd just finished the daily count

and was thinking how nice it would be to rest his bones for a while under the spreading branches of the terebinth tree, when he suddenly heard someone calling from further down the hillside.

'Joshua! Hey, Joshua!'

He recognized the voice immediately. 'Shalom, Hanani! Not often I see you up here. What a fine morning it is!'

'Fine morning it isn't!' puffed the friend he'd grown up with, and now was growing old with, his round face red and sweaty from the climb. 'You're supposed...' he stopped to gasp for breath, and sank his large, ungainly frame down under the inviting shade of the terebinth, 'you're supposed to be helping me mend my walls this morning. You've forgotten, I see!' He wagged a fat finger at Joshua, then wiped his brow. 'Heavens, but that hill gets steeper every year!'

'Ah—your walls! Yes, of course. I was just about to remember! It's just that my sheep...'

'Your sheep can manage without you for half an hour—they haven't the brains to do anything except stand in a huddle! Besides, Kenaz will watch them for you.' He waved his hand in the direction of his youngest son, a bare-headed, black-haired, bright-eyed lad, who was scrambling up the hill to join them.

Joshua sighed. He'd really rather stay with his precious flock. But, a promise was a promise, and he'd always prided himself on keeping his (though sometimes, these days, his memory let him down a bit). So, while Hanani waited impatiently, he gave the boy lengthy instructions about looking after the sheep, warning him of possible predators and making him repeat them, just as he'd done at a similar age. 'Here,' he added, 'keep my club by you, in case any wild animals approach!'

Kenaz looked doubtfully at the rather battered lump of wood and squinted up at Joshua. He didn't fancy his chances much against a bear with such a meagre weapon! He watched Joshua start to follow his father down the hillside, then turned and made a face at the sheep. 'Give me cattle any day!' he muttered to himself.

Suddenly he heard his name being called and turned

abruptly to see that Joshua had stopped at a point where the ground dipped downwards quite steeply (below which he knew he would lose sight of his flock). 'Hey, Kenaz,' Joshua was calling, 'did I mention scorpions?'

'You mentioned scorpions!' Hanani placed a hand firmly on Joshua's shoulder to propel him down the hill. 'Five times you mentioned scorpions!'

Joshua nodded. 'Thought so,' he said, taking one last look at his flock as they disappeared from view. Then, with a sigh, he carried on down the hillside.

It seemed to Paul that half the school was in the library! No chance of checking his cockroaches till after lessons. That bothered him all afternoon because, having had to close the tank up so hurriedly, he wasn't sure if he'd dropped the right cockroaches into the right sections. As soon as he could he returned to the lab, dragging along a very reluctant Nathan, and started checking the insects. They all appeared to be in their correct sections but, to his horror, he could find only twenty-four!

'Nathan!' he hissed. 'Count these cockroaches for me.'

'What?!' Nathan was aghast. Looking at them through glass was bad enough!

'I think one's missing! There should be twenty-five, but there's so much greenery in here it's hard to tell. Stick your hand in. See what you make it.'

'Er...' mumbled Nathan, taking several steps backwards.

'Oh, don't be a twit—they won't bite you!'

In the end, they compromised, and Paul moved them about with a stick while Nathan counted. 'Definitely twenty-four!' He frowned, glancing nervously at the floor. 'Er—if there should be twenty-five—where's the other one gone?'

'That's just the trouble. I don't know! Except it must still have been on my sleeve when I closed the tank up before going to the library. Rats!' Then, to Nathan's amazement, he got down on his hands and knees, and starting crawling round the edges of the room.

'Well, help me look!' he demanded, stopping mid-crawl beside Nathan's seriously scuffed shoes. 'It's black—about 30 millimetres long. Those ones don't fly, but they move pretty fast. He's probably in a dark corner somewhere. We've got to find him!'

'Why "we"?' Nathan frowned. He really quite fancied going home there and then, actually.

'Because it's important! He might get trodden on, get too cold, or not find enough to eat, and die. You'll have to help— everyone'll have to help!'

Nathan couldn't understand this at all. It was only a single rotten cockroach! It could look after itself, he'd have thought! 'Everyone?' he repeated incredulously.

'No! Hang on.' Paul sat back on his haunches. 'Best keep it quiet! Let's think.' He frowned. 'Can't let the teachers know there's a cockroach loose in the place. They mightn't be too impressed!'

'Exactly!' agreed Nathan eagerly. 'So let's just forget about it and go home!'

'So let's just stay here till we find him,' corrected Paul. 'It's the first one I ever hatched out. The first one I ever...' He nearly said, 'the first one I ever named'—Mad Max, because right from the start it'd charged around like a mad thing—but stopped himself just in time! 'Umm—the first one I ever saw shed a skin. Anyway, I like my cockroaches—every single one of them!' Nathan remained standing, decidedly unconvinced.

Paul sighed. A more persuasive tack was obviously needed! 'OK. What if he turns up in the school kitchen? What if he finds another cockroach in there, and starts mating, and the kitchens get overrun with baby cockroaches, and the Health and Hygiene people close the school down, and they'll know it's all my fault because I'm in charge of the tank, and then they'll expel me and I'll never get my exams, and not get into the RAF and never fly planes like I've wanted to my whole, entire life!'

He took a breath, visualizing the headlines in the local press: SCHOOLBOY STARTS COCKROACH EPIDEMIC! He stood up, placing a hand on Nathan's shoulder, and lowered his voice to as serious a tone as he could manage. 'You wouldn't want that on your conscience, now would you?'

Nathan wrinkled his nose and shook his head. 'Could it still have been on your sleeve when you left the lab?' he suggested.

'Maybe, yes—brilliant idea! He might have dropped off along the corridor. You look to the left, and I'll look to the right.' He headed out of the lab, and they both walked slowly down the corridor; Paul in desperate hopes he'd see his lost cockroach, and Nathan, on the whole, hoping he wouldn't!

They went on to search the library but there was still no sign of the insect. 'I'll get into trouble if I don't go home soon,' grumbled Nathan after nearly an hour. 'Besides, I'm starving hungry. Mum'd run out of bread this morning, so I couldn't have any sandwiches in my lunchbox. My stomach's been sounding like a...'

'Like a gorilla in pain! I know, I've been sitting next to it all afternoon! It's OK. You go. I'll stay a bit longer and have another hunt round the lab.'

They crept down a back route to the fire exit near the lab, avoiding those teachers still working. Banging the bar to open the door caused a loud metallic noise to echo along the corridor, and Nathan scuttled hurriedly outside. There were big, dark clouds moving fast overhead, making it look like evening already, and rain was beginning to fall in large, heavy drops.

'Told you it would rain!' Nathan pulled up his collar. 'Shall I tell Sam to leave going to the Clubhouse till tomorrow?'

'Suppose so, yes,' agreed Paul reluctantly. It was maddening, but he could only really think about finding Mad Max. 'I'll still try to get to Jessie's later, if I can.'

'I'll call by your house, too, if you like, and tell your mum you've got held up.'

'She probably won't be back yet, but Dad'll be in the surgery. Just leave a message with his receptionist.'

Nathan nodded, his stomach rumbling loudly. Paul pulled a chocolate bar out of his pocket and handed it to him. 'Here, for heaven's sake eat this! You sound revolting!'

'Hey, thanks!' Nathan took the bar gratefully and set off towards home, doing his best to avoid the puddles, because his shoes leaked and made his socks all soggy!

Paul closed the door and returned to the darkened lab. Using the neat little torch he always kept in his pocket, he meticulously shone it in every corner. He'd cared for those cockroaches ever since his dad had got hold of the eggs, keeping them in his bedroom, feeding them leftovers from his own plate, and watching them grow. They were fascinating—and they were his! He just hated the thought of losing any one of them.

Eventually, though, he gave up the search, creeping out into the pouring rain, hugely depressed and wishing he'd kept half the chocolate bar for himself! Ten minutes later, soaked through and squatting next to the boiler in the utility room, he glumly inspected the scrape on his shin he'd got slipping on a wet, muddy patch on the edge of the playground. Then, for the first time in his life, he muttered something approaching a prayer: 'If you're there, God, help me find Max tomorrow, huh? Jessie says you're always listening, so maybe you could prove it! Minor miracle stuff. How about it?'

The wall had taken a lot longer than half an hour to mend.

'Just like Hanani to underestimate these jobs!' Joshua muttered to himself as he climbed back up the hill. He looked up at the deeply blue sky and grinned. 'When you were dishing out optimism, Lord, Hanani went back for extra helpings, yes?'

He shielded his eyes from the bright, burning sun. It would be so good to feel some rain on his back for a change! As he reached the rise, and clambered up the familiar path, he got his first view of the flock. They were contentedly chewing grass, much as he'd left them two hours earlier, but somehow he just knew something wasn't right. And, what was more, he couldn't see Kenaz!

Joshua quickened his step, glancing anxiously around the hillside, and then suddenly noticed a huddled shape at the foot of the terebinth tree. It was Kenaz, stretched out on his back, snoring surprisingly loudly, black hair flopped across his face.

Joshua strode across to him and prodded him with his staff. 'Hey, you, wake up! You should be watching over my sheep, keeping them safe from attack, not dreaming!'

The boy sat up abruptly and scrambled to his feet. 'I'm sorry! I didn't mean to fall asleep. It was so hot, and you were such a long time. Please don't tell my father!' he pleaded. 'The sheep...' he looked anxiously towards the flock, 'they're quite all right. See?'

Joshua saw. Nothing looked different, and yet something was bothering him. 'You must help me count them.' He strode off towards his flock, quietly sounding the names of the ones he could immediately see.

'Count them?' Kenaz asked incredulously. He'd heard his father speak scathingly about sheep—how they hadn't the wit to do anything other than stare into space, endlessly chew grass, and then follow their leader home—and he'd automatically adopted the same opinion. 'What do we have to count them for?'

'Because some of them could easily have wandered off while you were dozing, that's why!'

'Oh, I'm sure none of them did!' Kenaz tried to sound confident.

'I hope you're right, young man! But, in the meantime, we count...'

'Ninety-nine,' Kenaz eventually exclaimed, pleased he'd been able to count so high. 'That's a lot of sheep!'

'Eve is missing!' The firstborn of his flock.

'Eve?' the boy repeated, his eyes widening. His father's friend named his sheep?!

'Never mind!' Joshua climbed the hill a little further to get a better look around. 'She must be found! You start looking in that direction,' he pointed to the east, 'and I'll go to the west.'

'But it's only one sheep!' Kenaz exclaimed. 'You've got ninety-nine others!'

Joshua didn't answer. He couldn't expect the boy to understand that it wouldn't have mattered if he'd had one thousand and ninety-nine, he'd still want to find the one that was lost.

'There are small caves to the east,' he said, pointing. 'I've known sheep wander into them before now, so keep the club. You never know what else might be hiding there!' Kenaz nodded and set off, not sure whether to be excited by that thought, or not.

'Silly sheep, where are you?' he muttered under his breath. 'What did you have to wander off for anyway?' In the distance he could see a stretch of cliff with dark patches in it. 'Caves. Great!' He quickened his pace.

Meanwhile, Joshua had come to a wide area scattered with large boulders, among which tall thorn bushes grew. He grinned to himself, showing several black teeth. 'Bet that's where my Eve is!' He started clambering over the rocks. 'Not past it yet!' he grunted, proud that in spite of his age (and not like Hanani, he thought, with a chuckle) he was still quite agile. However, in spite of a long search, he found no trace of his missing sheep, but plenty of sharp pieces of rock to stub his toes on and get his sandles caught between; not to mention the thorny bushes which seemed to reach out and grab him when he wasn't looking!

Across the other side of the hill, Kenaz had found every cave depressingly empty—not even any hyenas to scare off! He wandered further across the sun-drenched hill, even beginning to call out 'Eve! Eve!' (though he felt rather daft and was glad none of his friends were around to hear!) but it didn't help. Eventually he met up again with Joshua, who by now looked very hot, dirty, scratched and worried.

'No sign of her?' he asked anxiously.

The boy shook his head morosely and gazed up at the sky. He could tell by the position of the sun that it was past noon time, and by the rumbling of his stomach that it was past food time!

Joshua was hungry too but, feeling suddenly sorry for Kenaz, reached into his pouch and handed him the lump of barley bread he'd saved for later. 'Here, take this. You'll frighten away the rest of my sheep with such noises!' Kenaz took a bite gratefully.

'And now you'd better be getting home. Your mother will be wondering where you've got to. I shall tell your father you searched well, and that it wasn't your fault. That sheep is always wandering off. She's what you'd call adventurous! Tell him I shall continue searching until I find her—however long it takes. Oh,' he added, 'and you'd better break the news to my dear wife, too!'

Kenaz made a face and Joshua laughed. 'It's all right! Her bark's worse than her bite!'

The boy nodded, though he wasn't convinced! He scampered down the hill, Joshua watching him for a moment or two before beginning his search again.

The sun was now hotter than ever and, an hour later, losing his footing on a particularly steep piece of rock, Joshua slid and landed in a heap in the middle of a sprawling, spiky bush. 'I'm getting too old for this!' he groaned, inspecting his scraped shin. Then, because only God was around to hear, he called out, 'Lord, I know you're listening! How about a little help to find my sheep? That shouldn't be too difficult since you already know where she is! Point me in the right direction—preferably avoiding all the thorn bushes! Just a little miracle, huh?!'

Paul hardly slept that night. When he eventually dozed off, he dreamt he'd turned into a brown beetle, and was crawling around the playground on his stomach, desperately trying to avoid the feet of giant children clumping around above him. It was a relief to wake up and get to school!

He met up with Nathan and Sam by the gates. Nathan looked a little more cheerful (but just as scruffy!) as the previous day and Sam was grinning broadly, her green eyes sparkling mischievously.

'Hey! Guess what's for lunch today, Paul?' she chortled. 'Cockroach soup. Tasty!'

'Ha, ha, very funny!'

'Jessie suggested you print out a "Reward" poster on your computer. You know the sort of thing: "Lost Cockroach. Wanted for Looking Disgusting. Capture Dead or Alive!"'

'Yes, I saw Jessie last night, too.' Paul sighed. 'Nice to find my friends are so sympathetic!'

'Touching, really!' Sam nodded. 'Makes a change for you to do something wrong.'

'I didn't! It was Miss Grant's fault, actually.'

'So you both got to see Jessie, then?' asked Nathan.

'I called round after tennis practice to take her some magazines, and some more of my mum's famous herbal remedy,' nodded Sam. 'She said she was feeling a bit better, but I don't think she'll be back today, lucky thing!'

'You must've left just before I got there. I took her some CDs, and let her borrow my player. Of course!' he suddenly clicked his fingers together. 'Your herbal stuff! She must've already had some of it and that was what was making her delirious!'

'Delirious? She wasn't delirious!'

'Definitely was! What does your mum put in that stuff? You ought to be careful, you know!'

'Don't talk rubbish!' Sam laughed, leading the way into school.

'Well, she said my lost cockroach was really a lost sheep, and that Luke knew all about it. If that isn't delirious, I don't know what is!'

'Who's Luke?'

'Search me! She said it was a riddle.'

'Apart from being batty, what's actually the matter with her?' asked Nathan, grinning. 'She said the other night it wasn't flu. Thought she'd be better by now.'

Sam shrugged. 'Caught some sort of bug, I suppose. There's a lot of it about.'

'Hey, maybe she's got the cockroach!' Nathan suddenly chortled. The others looked at him blankly. 'Bug—cockroach—get it?' Well, he thought it was funny!

'Wish she had,' groaned Paul. 'It's Combined Sciences first thing this morning. Old Deakin asked me yesterday morning how many cockroaches there were at the moment, 'cos he wants them out for the class today. He'll go spare if one's missing. Help me look, after Register, will you?'

They each hunted in different places, without any luck, managing to sit themselves down in the lab only moments before the Science teacher entered.

Mr Deakin, bald, thin and severe, strode abruptly into the room and stood with hands behind his back, feet well apart. His lips curled in a mean Deakin-smile. 'This morning,' he said, peering at them through thick-lensed glasses and moving slowly round the class, 'you'll be studying the intriguing world of insects. And don't,' he twirled round abruptly, 'let me hear so much as a squirm out of any of you!'

He strode back to his desk. 'As you know, Bridges has brought a collection of twenty-five cockroaches into the lab, which he will now proceed to wheel to the front of the class.' He expected Paul to jump up and immediately follow his instructions. To his annoyance, though, Paul just sat, seemingly fascinated by the floor. 'Bridges!' Mr Deakin barked.

'What? Oh, sorry, Mr Deakin. Were you speaking to me?'
'The tank! I require it moved up here.'
'Er... now?'
'Of course now!'

Paul rose slowly to his feet, appeared to sway for a moment, holding his stomach as if in extreme pain, then with a loud groan collapsed on to the floor. 'What the blazes are you doing, Bridges?' Mr Deakin thundered. 'Get up at once!'

Nathan, whose survival policy usually was to be as unnoticeable as possible, nevertheless jumped down from his stool and crouched beside Paul. 'What's the matter?' he whispered, looking worried.

'My cockroach—that's what's the matter!' Paul hissed in his ear. 'It's on Deakin's right shoe! It'll be climbing up his trouser leg next!'

'What! How did it get there?'

'I don't know! What were you saying yesterday about there being no tornadoes? If Deakin feels it crawling up him there'll be a tornado, all right, and I'll be in the middle of it!'

Mr Deakin by this time had moved to where Paul lay in a crumpled heap. He towered over him, tapping his foot in annoyance, while the cockroach, using the highly efficient spines on its legs, crawled relentlessly up his shoelaces. Paul gave another agonized groan, going for maximum effect, and vaguely wondered whether he should abandon the Air Force idea and go for acting instead!

Nathan, with a rare flash of inspiration, said, 'He's not been feeling well all week, Mr Deakin. It's this bug that's going round.'

Sam, who just at that moment had noticed the black, shiny cockroach creeping up the teacher's grey sock, started giggling uncontrollably. 'That's right!' she spluttered. 'A really nasty, big bug!'

And then Paul suddenly lurched forward in a coughing fit, seemingly so violent that he had to support himself on Mr Deakin's smart, shiny shoes...

The teacher withdrew his feet with distaste. 'Stand up!' he hissed. 'You're making an exhibition of yourself. Get a drink from the back of the lab and pull yourself together. Then you—and Norstadt—bring the trolley with the cockroaches up to the front. And,' he glared around the room, 'no further interruptions, or you'll all be staying behind after school tonight!'

The class, who knew to their cost that he didn't make idle

threats, stared studiously forward, so didn't really notice Paul get up, wink at Sam, and make his way to the back of the room—bent over, just for good measure, as though still in pain. With Nathan's help, he took the lid off the tank and opened his hand, gently dropping Mad Max back into the tank to join his companions. Paul grinned from ear to ear.

'My lost cockroach,' he whispered. 'Safe and sound! A miracle, or what?!'

There's almost no twilight in countries like Israel. One minute it's broad daylight, then, very nearly the next, it's dark. Joshua, not having found Eve, had been forced to give up the search for the night. But he didn't want to go down off the hill with the rest of the flock in case his precious sheep might suddenly return. Miracles like that had happened before!

His *himation* (the thick woollen cloak shepherds always wore) acted as a warm blanket, and some of it he pulled up under his head so he could lie more comfortably on the hard, dry ground. But he was restless and found it difficult to sleep. When he finally dozed off, it was to dream that he was a boy again, fighting off a pack of wolves that were stronger and more ferocious than any he'd had to deal with in real life. His flock of sheep was enormous, covering the whole of the hillside, and when he woke up with the dawn it was a relief to discover it had only been a dream!

Joshua stretched his aching limbs and gazed up at the cloudless sky. 'Sorry to trouble you so early, Lord,' he said, 'but my Eve is still missing. Of course, of course,' he nodded, 'you know that. But a little reminder…?'

Joshua never doubted his prayers were heard, but even he was stunned when, only twenty minutes later, he suddenly heard the unmistakable sound of bleating from beyond a place where the rocks had fallen away to leave a sheer drop down to the next valley. He'd passed the spot the day before, but had heard nothing then. He got down on his stomach, wriggling cautiously towards the edge. And there to his amazement was Eve, standing on a small ledge against a thin

but sturdy tree that stubbornly clung to the rock. It was the only thing preventing the animal from toppling over into the valley far below.

Joshua didn't know whether to be happy or terrified! He stood up awkwardly, knowing he would have to get help—and fast. He hurried back to the rest of his flock, checked they were safe, then made his way down the hill. Even from quite a distance he could see Hanani, walking behind his ox, ploughing a field and planting his wheat, so he headed as quickly as he could in that direction. As he got closer he could see that Kenaz was also there, following the plough and removing weeds with a hoe.

'Hanani, friend—I need your help—urgently!' he yelled, waving and pointing up towards the hills.

'Not that sheep of yours?' Hanani called back, pulling his ox to a halt.

'Stuck on a ledge. I need rope, and Kenaz!'

Hanani cupped his hands to his mouth so his words would carry better. 'Kenaz will bring rope. I'll follow as soon as I've secured my ox.'

Joshua waved his acknowledgment, and waited as patiently as he could—which wasn't very!—till the boy, a large circle of thick rope around his shoulder, scrambled up to join him.

'She's alive then?' Kenaz asked, finding, to his surprise, that he cared.

'Yes, but we must hurry,' replied Joshua.

Together they made their way towards the edge of the cliff. Glancing quickly down, and relieved to see Eve still on the ledge, Joshua went over to a nearby boulder, securing the rope around it. Kenaz then led the rope around a small tree further along, Joshua dropping the remaining length over the cliff, near to the ledge.

'Well, it should have been longer, but it'll have to do,' he said, peering over the edge. He looked at Kenaz. 'I'm definitely too old for the next bit!'

'That's all right,' grinned the boy, enthusiastically. 'I can get down there easily!'

'Not until your father is here! Go back to the flock, wait for him, then bring him here.'

Joshua again did his best to be patient, pulling the rope back up so it could be tied around the boy's waist, and eventually was able to watch Kenaz edging his way down the cliff-face towards Eve. The sheep began bleating even more pitifully. Kenaz dropped nimbly down on to the ledge and waved up at Joshua and his father, grinning broadly.

'The boy thinks it's a game!' grumbled Hanani.

'It is, to him!' remarked Joshua. 'Undo the rope, Kenaz, and tie it around her body, just behind the front legs,' he instructed. 'Fine! Now guide her up as we pull.'

Sheep are pretty heavy things, and it took a fair amount of effort for the two men to haul her up. When at last they managed to drag her over the top she just lay on the ground, confused and seemingly unable to move. Joshua undid the rope carefully, whispering quietly in her ear and gently checking to see if the animal was injured in any way. Hanani quickly threw the rope back over the cliff, saw that Kenaz had tied it around himself, then began pulling his son to safety.

Kenaz had just got to his feet and untied the rope when the sheep, very abruptly, scrambled to her feet also. The boy, with a big grin, went over to her, sinking his fingers into her long fleece. 'Well, you look just fine! Thought you'd be there for ever, didn't you, Eve?' he laughed.

'Eve?' Hanani queried, frowning. He turned to Joshua, 'In all the heavens, you surely don't have names for them, too?'

'Who, me?!' Joshua raised his eyebrows as if with amazement at the very suggestion! Then, with more strength than he realized he still had, swept his precious lost sheep up on to his shoulder and, with the greatest delight, carried her all the way back to join the rest of the flock.

Joshua grinned from ear to ear. 'Thank you, Lord,' he chortled, as he placed Eve gently on the ground. 'My lost sheep! Safe and sound! That's what I call a miracle!'

Later that afternoon, inside their impressive Clubhouse (which was, as Paul had predicted, perfectly dry) Nathan, Sam and Jessie (now well enough to join them) celebrated with Paul the safe return of his precious lost cockroach.

He was just handing Jessie a can of fizzy drink when he

had a sudden thought. 'Hey, I figured out your riddle, by the way,' he said.

'Knew you would!' She nestled her back into a corner of the treehouse, stretching her long legs out. 'You're just so amazingly clever!'

'Brilliant!' agreed Sam.

'Incredible, really!' chortled Nathan.

'Glad you realize this!' Paul stuck his fingers in imaginary lapels and strutted about grandly. 'It was simple really—for a highly superior brain like mine!'

'Oh, get on with it!' Sam stuck out a foot, nearly tripping Paul up, and he turned on her, grinning, skimming a hand over her tightly cropped, dark-ginger hair. She ducked out of the way, giggling. 'Come on. Tell! What was the riddle? I know you said something about it this morning, but I've forgotten.'

'I said he hadn't lost a cockroach, he'd lost a sheep, and he'd find out all about it from Luke,' said Jessie, propping her hands behind her head.

'Luke who?' asked Nathan, confused.

'Luke chapter fifteen, verses one to seven,' quoted Paul smugly. 'Found it in the school library Bible. It's a story about a shepherd who's got a hundred sheep, but loses one and spends ages searching for it. Then, when he finds it, he has a party to celebrate. Knew it had to be something to do with church, coming from Jessie!'

'Doesn't have to be!' she said defensively. She was the only one in the gang who regularly went to church, and didn't talk about it much at school, in case of getting teased.

'Anyway, I was right, wasn't I?' Paul sat himself down next to her triumphantly. 'I'll tell you what, though, that story must've been about my cockroach, too—not just about a dirty great sheep!'

'Oh yes!' laughed Jessie. 'How do you figure that one out?'

'Well, I found another version of that story in Matthew, and that says that God "doesn't want any of these little ones to be lost". Now who on earth would call sheep "little"? My cockroach, on the other hand... he's definitely little!'

'Isn't—it's huge!' protested Sam, stuffing her mouth full of crisps.

'Doesn't mean either,' said Jessie. 'It's a parable.'

'What's a parable?' asked Nathan, taking a bite out of his third chocolate bar.

'A story that explains one thing by talking about another. Jesus used them all the time.'

'Oh, well, he would, wouldn't he!' Sam grinned.

'What he meant,' went on Jessie, ignoring her, 'was that, just like the shepherd, God cares about every single one of us, no matter who we are.' She finished her drink with a loud guzzling noise. 'Just like Paul and his adorable cockroaches, really!'

'Sounds fair enough to me!' Paul laughed, getting to his feet and raising his can with a flourish. 'A toast!' he said grandly, looking round at his friends' smiling faces and remembering how great it had felt to see Mad Max safely back in the tank. 'To a day which has been, without question, the best one of my entire life—so far!'

That evening Joshua sat on the ground beside a large, open fire, the sky above filled with stars. His one hundred sheep were safely secured in the fold beside his house, and the sound of their soft bleating mingled pleasantly with the crackling of the burning wood. Miriam sat beside him, spreading thin pieces of dough on to the top of a large, shallow, earthenware bowl, which she'd placed upside-down over part of the fire. Fish was cooking in a pot of water, hanging over the remaining, uncovered flames.

'You've invited how many?' she asked sharply, distinctly annoyed at all the extra cooking she was having to do. Typical of Joshua to want to give a party just because he'd found a sheep that hadn't had the sense to stay with the rest of the flock in the first place!

'Oh, everyone!' Joshua couldn't help smiling at her aghast expression. 'Don't worry, my dear! They'll bring their own food.'

'And wine, I trust! We have one jug from the vineyard

along the valley, but that won't go far if Hanani comes along!'

'Of course Hanani will join us—and Kenaz, too. I want them all to celebrate with me the return of my precious lost sheep.'

'And I suppose all the other boys will expect to come, if he does!'

'Nonsense!' he laughed. 'Anyway, he deserves to be allowed to join in such an occasion as this!'

'He certainly does!' Kenaz suddenly appeared round the side of their small house and plumped himself down on the ground, grinning up at Joshua and nodding politely to Miriam, who shook her head and tutted loudly.

'I suppose, between the two of you, you could just about manage to keep an eye on the bread, and make sure it doesn't wander off?' she muttered, and disappeared inside the house to get the wine. When she came out again a few moments later, it was to see all their relations, friends and neighbours—about thirty, in all—gathering with Joshua around the fire, laughing and joking.

'We have fish cooking here, and loaves, as you can see,' Joshua was saying, 'and, of course, the wine!' He held out his drinking cup, which Hanani filled from the jug his own wife had brought over.

'Drink a toast with me, my friends,' he announced, raising his cup and looking round at their smiling faces, remembering the great joy he'd felt on returning Eve safely to the rest of his flock. 'For this has been, without question, the best day of my entire life!'

A.S.L.T.W!

Fairview Secondary's school band may not have been the most tuneful in the county, but what it lacked in talent it made up for with enthusiasm! Mr Pettifer, the Music teacher, was immensely proud of it, anyway. Nothing like music for raising everyone's spirits, he always thought.

It wasn't actually a very big band, because those in it were having to give up two lunch breaks a week (extra practice because of the End of Summer Term Concert coming up for parents and the rest of the school) and not everyone thought it worth the sacrifice!

Then, to make matters worse, a fortnight before the concert, a flu epidemic hit the school (typical!) and each day more and more children were absent through illness. Which meant the band was rapidly getting smaller and smaller! It was a serious problem.

By the time another week had passed, Mr Pettifer decided urgent measures were needed! He began going round each of the classes to make 'An Important Announcement'.

'As you might know,' he began, standing at the front of Miss Grant's class, 'due to the—um—unfortunate illness some of our pupils are suffering from, the School Band is urgently in need of extra players for the concert next week.' He dabbed his round, shiny forehead with a damp-looking handkerchief. Prone to perspiring rather a lot, it hadn't taken

Sam long to dub Mr Pettifer 'Mr Sweatyfer'!

'I'm going to individually ask those of you who play instruments, but haven't yet joined the band, if you will—um—help us out on this Important Occasion.' Mr Pettifer smiled encouragingly. 'It will entail giving up—um—several break-times, of course, including this lunch break, but you should have your instruments with you today anyway, and it's a small price to pay for—um—Saving the Day, isn't it?'

Sam listened to all this and sighed deeply. She played the cornet (more loudly than well!) but she'd never actually wanted to join the band. She thought the music they played was just too boring for words! Besides, she certainly didn't want to give up any breaks! The weather had just turned really warm, and she loved being out of doors more than anything else.

Anyway, she'd arranged with Paul to practise some tennis strokes at lunch-time and, as far as she was concerned, that was definitely more important! She watched Mr Pettifer out of the corner of her eye, talking to others in the class, and buried her head in her book, hoping he'd forget she was there. No such luck!

'Well, Samantha,' he said quietly in her ear, not noticing her screw up her face in annoyance at the use of her full name. 'I'm sure you'd like to help, wouldn't you? We really do need everyone we can get, and you're a very—um—strong player.' He nodded his head and mopped his brow. 'Can I count on your being—um—with us?'

Paul grinned as he noticed Sam put on an impressively regretful expression. 'I'm really sorry, Mr Pettifer,' she said, 'but I've got to practise my tennis at lunch-time—for the school team, you know—and, well,' she shrugged, unable to resist saying what she really meant, 'I'd just prefer to do that, that's all.'

Not far outside Nazareth was a large and thriving vineyard, from where Joshua's celebratory jar of wine had come. It was owned by a jovial, roly-poly sort of man named Amos, who had three joys in his life: growing grapes and his two sons.

'Fine boys!' he would tell anyone who cared to listen. 'How they've cared for their old father since their mother died a year past—you can't imagine! God was good when he gave me such sons!' He loved them, pretty much as well as Joshua loved his sheep—which was saying quite a lot!

Very early on this particular day Amos was out checking his vines. Being early August, some grapes had already been picked and dried for the women to make raisin cakes, while more were in the vats, fermenting nicely. A lot were simply eaten while being picked! Right now, what concerned Amos most were his very best vines. These grew a little separately from the others and, even at a distance, you could see the grapes hanging more heavily than the rest. They were exactly ready for picking, the juicy fruit promising some very fine wine indeed.

'The finest!' he said proudly, picking a single grape and popping it into his mouth.

Grapes are pretty fragile things. Amos looked up at the hazy sky, mopping his brow with his sleeve. He could tell it was going to be hotter than hot, and if these grapes didn't get picked that day they'd ripen just that little too much. And the wine they'd make would be just that little less good. And a little less good wasn't good enough, as far as Amos was concerned! And here is where Amos had a problem.

'Have I got a problem!' he said out loud to anyone around who might be listening. Which was the problem—there was no one there to listen! Where regular, skilled workers would help him prune the vines earlier in the year, harvest time usually brought in lots of casual workers and, though the work was hard, it was a satisfying, cheerful kind of a job. Nothing like a good harvest to raise everyone's spirits, he always thought. Especially his own!

But this season a mysterious illness had spread through the villages, making him short of help all week, and today, so far, no one had turned up at all. It was a very serious situation. Amos shielded his eyes and looked along the path leading to the nearest village. He could just make out two figures approaching.

'Ay, yi, yi. Two—just two!' he muttered, walking along the path to meet them. 'Is there no one else coming?'

'Not this morning. Perhaps later.' Thomas, the tallest of the men, waved a hand towards the vineyard. 'Fine grapes, Amos!'

'Today—perfect,' he agreed, spreading his hands. 'Tomorrow—who knows? But, you're here, so we must be thankful.' He tried to look cheerful. 'The baskets are ready. You make a start and I'll go and find my sons. As soon as they know the problem, they'll lend a hand, for sure.'

Thomas thought it more likely that, as usual, neither would be willing to help, but resisted the temptation to say so! Amos hurried off, mopping his brow again, from both the gradually increasing heat and the worry. He headed for the rear of the house where he remembered earlier seeing Joash (eighteen, tall and proud), sitting on the back step, mending a fishing-net.

He was still there. 'Ah, Joash!' He plopped himself heavily down beside his son. 'Such good fortune to find you still here! Have I got a job for you!'

Joash didn't answer. Never a good sign. Amos put an arm around his son's shoulder. 'Now,' he said encouragingly, 'you know there is this illness going around—such an illness!—and only two men have arrived this morning.'

'Er—vaguely remember you mentioning it.' Joash held up the area of net he was working on. 'Does this look all right to you? It got torn on a rock last time I used it.'

Amos waved a hand in the air. What did he know about fishing-nets! 'Fine,' he said, 'it looks fine, but Joash, listen to me. The grapes must be picked today. I badly need your help.'

Joash put the net down and sighed deeply. When would his father get the message! He was always trying to get him to work in the vineyard—the eldest son inheriting the family business, and all that—but a fisherman was all he'd ever wanted to be.

Joash picked up a square of cloth and a length of plaited wool, wound both deftly around his head to protect himself from the sun, and stood up. 'I'm sorry, but my friends are expecting me,' he said. 'We're casting from the shore first, then going out on a boat tonight, so don't expect me back till tomorrow.'

He gathered together the net, pushing it into a large goatskin bag. Amos stood up to help him. 'It's all right. I can manage,' Joash muttered, swinging the bag over his shoulder. 'I'm sorry you're short of helpers but I've told you before, I really don't want to work in the vineyard.'

Jessie was a good clarinet player. She practised hard and occasionally got up the courage to accompany a song in church, which invariably would be one her mother insisted on singing! Jessie's family originated in Jamaica, where just about everyone sang—usually pretty well, and Jessie's mum thought she was no exception. However, 'singing' wasn't quite the term most people gave to the sounds she produced! Their diplomatic comments usually consisted of 'Unique' and 'What a voice!' and 'I've never heard anything like it!' and she would go home thrilled with the compliments. Jessie kept the subject of her going to church each week fairly quiet at school, but unfortunately couldn't keep her mum's singing quiet!

Jessie hadn't got around to joining the band, though

she'd been meaning to for a long while, if only because Nathan played the saxophone in it (not badly, as it happened). But, somehow, she never seemed to remember band practice until it was too late.

She glanced up from her essay as Mr Pettifer approached her desk, and immediately felt sorry for him. Normally he was one of those permanently jolly people. Right now, he looked extremely worried.

He bent down towards her, mopped his brow, and tried to look cheerful. 'Encouragement—that's my motto in life,' he would say to anyone who cared to listen.

'Well, Jessica,' he said quietly, 'your mother's always telling me how—um—splendidly you play your clarinet in church, and I'm sure you realize how important it is to have our best players in the band. We'd really—um—value your presence, you know.'

Jessie felt surprised and pleased at his comments, and gave him one of her broadest smiles. 'Yes, of course I'll help—I'd like to! I've got to finish something for my art project straight after lunch, but that won't take long, and then I promise I'll come over to the hall.'

'Splendid! Good girl!' Mr Pettifer said delightedly, moving on to the next child on his list, and hoping Jessie's enthusiasm was at least as contagious as the flu!

Amos watched Joash walk away and felt greatly depressed. If his wife had still been alive he was sure she'd have managed to persuade him to help. She'd been good at that sort of thing.

Still, all was not lost! 'Nahash won't let me down,' he muttered to himself, trying to lift his spirits. 'That is,' he looked upwards, 'if you can please tell me, Lord, where he's hiding himself today?!'

Nahash, three years younger than Joash, and taking after his father in looks and temperament, nevertheless had one particular tendency inherited from his mother: never to be where one expected him to be! Amos, out of habit, looked for him in the unexpected places first, only to find him eventually amongst the olive trees, in the middle of which was the well. 'Wouldn't you know it,' Amos muttered to himself. 'Collecting water—just exactly what he should be doing this time of the morning!'

He walked over to the well, dipped his hand into the leather bucket and splashed the cool water over his face. 'Just what I needed!' he exclaimed, beaming at Nahash. 'That's much better! Now, I have a job for you, my son. An urgent job! I need you to...'

'Help collect in the grapes?' Nahash interrupted with a grin, pouring the water from the bucket into a couple of earthenware jars—women's work that his mother certainly would have been doing if she'd still been alive. 'I saw you were a bit short of workers. Do you need help straight away?'

'Straight away would be good!' Amos answered delightedly. 'With this wretched illness going around I don't know if anyone else'll turn up today. Will you come?'

'Of course!' Nahash answered. 'Happy to. I've been meaning to start helping you for ages, anyway.' He lifted up the two large jars and headed towards the welcome shade of the house. 'I'll just get these inside and clear up a few things. Then I'll be there. I promise!'

After she'd had lunch—her favourite pizza and chips, followed by strawberry mousse—Jessie went straight to the art block. One of the best in her year at all kinds of art, she'd been specially working on a scaled-down replica of an ancient Israeli wine jar, with a funny name she could never remember. She'd chosen this particular thing to do because the shape fascinated her: tall and narrow, with a long pointed end which would have been pushed deep into earth or sand to keep the wine cool. She'd just finished painting a few lines around the top for decoration when a girl from the next year up, whose parents were also Jamaican, literally crashed into the room.

Jessie, spinning round and almost sending the jar flying, cried, 'Oh, Maddy! You made me jump!'

'Sorry!' the older girl grinned. 'Tripped on something—don't know what! Must've been these glasses.'

'You tripped on your glasses?'

'No, idiot! I've got new specs, and I really don't think they're working very well!' She pulled the thick-lensed glasses off her nose and rubbed them vigorously on the hem of her dress. 'Anyway, found you, didn't I?'

Jessie grinned. Maddy Jenkins might be a year older than her, but certainly never seemed like it! 'Yup! I'm definitely here!' she teased. 'What's the problem—apart from the glasses, I mean?'

'No problem.' Maddy sat her rather large self down on one of the tables, nearly sending the pot of paint Jessie had been using toppling on to the floor. 'Whoops! What a daft place to leave paint!'

'Completely stupid!' agreed Jessie, quickly rescuing it.

'OK, now. Remember that magazine I was telling you about last week?'

'The one your cousin in Kingston gets?'

'Precisely! Well…' She produced from behind her back, with a flourish, a glossy colour magazine. 'It's got some great stuff in it! Lots of arty things—just up your street. Do you want to come outside and see?'

'Love to! I've done all I can here now, anyway. Just let me put my things away…'

'I'll help!' Maddy leapt up, sending an easel clattering to the floor.

'No, don't! Er—I mean, that's OK. I can manage!' Jessie hurriedly tidied up, carefully placing the wine holder back on its shelf out of harm's way, then followed Maddy outside to where they could sit comfortably on the grass. The lunch break drifted along pleasantly and quickly, with band practice a long way from Jessie's mind.

Meanwhile, Mr Pettifer, trying hard to encourage and organize the few new players who had turned up, mopped his brow for the twentieth time. He felt very disappointed at not seeing Jessie there. She was such a good clarinet player. And she'd promised.

Out in the vineyard, Amos mopped his brow. The baskets of grapes were filling up, but all too slowly. He put a hand up to his eyes to shield them from the sun, and peered towards the house. Still no sign of Nahash! He was deeply disappointed. The lad was a good worker—when he could be

persuaded to turn up. And he'd promised.

'Expect he's found something else to do that he thinks is more important!' Thomas grunted, being careful not to let Amos hear.

'Or preferred to stay in the cool!' the other man muttered in annoyance.

Meanwhile, Nahash was having a bit of a problem! It wasn't that he hadn't understood how much his help was needed out in the vineyard. He certainly had. And he knew he ought to be out there already. But there was something on his mind that morning—and it wasn't grapes!

You see, Nahash was really a potter. At least, that's how he liked to think of himself. He'd started making jugs and jars for his father's wine a couple of years previously—just because it was more convenient than bringing them in from the village all the time, but lately he'd been making many more things: bowls, lamps, drinking-cups. Then, just that week, he'd made up his mind to try his hand at making an amphora: the tall, narrow, pointed-ended vessel in which they stored the wine, pushing it deep into the ground in the most shady spot they could find. And that was his problem—he just hadn't been able to get the correct shape of those amphorae! They were so tall that they'd wobble all over the place on the wheel, no matter what speed he turned it. He'd been trying all week to get it right, but hadn't managed it yet. It was infuriating!

He'd been on his way out to the vineyard (really he had!) but had had to pass the small stone barn, where, at the age of thirteen and with his mother's help, he'd proudly set up his 'Pottery'. Somehow, he just couldn't quite resist diverting his steps to go in. It was cool inside and smelt wonderfully of clay. In the centre was a foot-operated wheel. 'Just a few minutes, that's all,' he said to himself. 'I'll just see if I can manage one amphora, and then I'll go and help with the grapes.'

Two hours later, he was very proudly looking at a couple of passably good amphorae, and feeling pretty pleased with himself, when he suddenly remembered something else.

'The toys!' he exclaimed out loud. 'I promised to make some toys for the village children. What was it they wanted? Oh, I know—horses and camels for the boys—and...' he picked up a small lump of clay and started moulding it in his hand, 'a few dolls and sheep for the girls, I think.' This was a lot easier to do, totally absorbing, and actually quite good fun!

At some point during the day, when he started on making tiny items for the miniature houses so popular with some of the village children, he did vaguely think he ought to be out helping his father. 'I know I said I'd be there,' he reasoned with himself, 'but I expect they're managing just fine without me.'

So, in spite of his promise, Nahash never did go and help in the vineyard that day.

After lunch Sam went thankfully out into the sunshine. She'd changed into gym things and was looking forward to practising her tennis strokes. She liked all sports, but loved tennis best. Apart from anything else, it was the only thing she was better at than any of her four brothers! And she'd been told that if she practised hard, there was every chance she'd get into the school team—which was certainly more than they'd ever managed!

Walking past the hall she heard, through the open windows, the band playing. They sounded remarkably not too bad, considering how few there were in there! A very slight feeling of guilt began to niggle her, but she put her head down and walked on resolutely. She was not going to help out with the concert. She had more important things to do!

'I suppose I could practise after school instead,' she muttered to herself, 'but that's not the point!' She walked on a bit further. 'And I know they need good players like me…' She lifted up her head, and threw back her shoulders proudly. 'A strong player—that's what Sweatyfer called me!' Two other girls walking past started to giggle. She ignored them. 'But I can't do everything, can I?' she thought.

And so she argued with herself, while herself argued back! This went on till she reached the courts where a couple of others were already playing a game. Paul, waiting in the next court, was absorbed in watching them. She loved the sound of the ball being hit and couldn't wait to start playing. The concert, she decided, would just have to go on without her. Definitely! Probably!

'Hi!' she called. 'Do hope I've kept you waiting! I'll serve first, OK?'

Paul nodded and hit a few of the balls into her side of the court. She picked up one, bounced it a couple of times, then threw it high up into the air. It was only actually at the point of automatically judging the moment she would bring round her racket to make her first serve that Sam finally came to a decision.

'Oh bother!' she exclaimed with annoyance, letting the ball drop to the ground and catching it deftly with one hand as it bounced. 'It's no good! I can't practise now. I'm going to have to help out with the band instead!'

'What?' Paul straightened up, frowning. 'I thought you didn't care about the concert?'

'Yeah, well, a leopard can change its skin, can't it?' she shrugged.

'Spots, actually!'

'What?'

'A leopard can't change its spots!'

'Right—that's what I said!' Sam hit the ball hard over the net. She turned and began to run out of the court, calling, 'Practise for me. Make sure I serve brilliantly!'

A few minutes later, walking nonchalantly into the hall as though she always played her cornet wearing gym shorts, she was welcomed warmly by Mr Pettifer.

'Come in, Samantha,' he called. 'Better late than never, eh? Knew you wouldn't let us down!

Joash took a short cut across his father's land towards the place where he'd arranged to meet his friends. It took him around the edge of the vineyard and, in the distance, he could see his father, with Thomas working beside him. There looked to be a huge number of vines as yet untouched. 'They'll be lucky to pick half the grapes by sunset, let alone all of them,' he thought to himself.

On the rare occasions when he'd helped in the past—and that was not for a long time—he'd found the work tedious in the extreme, though he had to admit the grapes had tasted good! He felt a tinge of guilt that he wasn't over there helping but, after all, it wasn't his fault the crop had ripened on the one day he'd arranged to do something else important!

He was so lost in thought that he jumped several handspans into the air when one of his friends suddenly came up behind him and clapped a hand on his back. 'Shalom, Joash! I could have stolen your bag and you wouldn't have noticed!'

'Abner! Are you coming too? Even better!'

'Wouldn't miss it! Haven't we been waiting since for ever to experience some real fishing, on a proper boat, instead of just standing on the shore and throwing our nets into the water?'

'Ah, you just don't like doing it that way because you have no muscles!' laughed Joash. 'Whereas I…' he held up an arm and made a show of strength, 'I am more than strong enough to cast my net into deep, deep waters.'

'And get it caught on big, big rocks! I saw the mess you'd made of your net last time!'

Joash grimaced and nodded.

'I'm surprised you're coming with us today, though,' Abner continued. 'I'd heard your father is very short of workers, with this strange illness going around. My uncle was well enough today to get out there, and my sister might make it later. He tried to persuade me, of course, but I said you'd be sure to be helping, what with it being your vineyard, and everything.'

'It's not my vineyard!' Joash stopped in his tracks, suddenly angry. 'And I'd rather fish! Everyone knows I'd rather fish!'

'Sure, fine—calm down. I was only saying…'

'Well don't!'

'No. Right!'

The two of them continued on in silence, Joash grimly determined not to feel in the least bit guilty and trying not to remember how worried his father had looked that morning. However, by the time he'd reached the rest of his waiting friends, he just knew that a great day and night's fishing was not what he was going to be able to allow himself, after all.

He stopped in the middle of the path and turned to Abner. 'Well—you're right, I suppose. I'm sorry,' he said to the rest of them, 'My father needs my help today. You're just going to have to fish without me.' He threw them the bag with the mended net. 'Here! Catch some big ones for me!'

A few minutes later, swinging a collecting-basket on to his back, he strode through the rows of vines towards Amos.

Catching sight of his eldest son, he called out, 'Joash—welcome! Knew you'd turn up in the end!'

To Sam's surprise, it wasn't half as boring playing with the band as she'd expected. Mr Pettifer's enthusiasm was somehow contagious, and it wasn't long before everyone was convinced they could each play brilliantly!

'It was actually pretty good!' she admitted, sitting up in the Clubhouse after school with Paul, waiting for the other two to join them. The treehouse had improved a lot since Paul had first slid down the rope on the day he'd lost his cockroach. Now there was rush matting on the floor, windchimes hanging outside the tent-flap door, a small, low table Paul had brought out of his own bedroom, a brightly coloured rug hanging on one wall, and a small cupboard, in which they hid sweets and other goodies.

'He had us playing one thing ever so quietly at the beginning,' Sam went on, grinning. 'Not easy, I can tell you! And then suddenly we had to go really loud. It was great!'

'Well, you'd certainly have had no problem doing the loud bit!' laughed Paul. 'You and Jessie's mum ought to get together. I don't know who makes the worst noise!'

Sam made a face. 'Beast! Sweatyfer was very complimentary about my playing, I'll have you know. He said he was extremely glad to have me join them. So there!'

'Always thought he must be half deaf, teaching you lot!' Paul teased. 'Anyway, talking of joining things, did I tell you I'm starting up a Young Entomologists Group?'

Sam looked at him blankly. 'Entomology,' he repeated. 'Come on! That's the science of insects. Everyone knows that!'

'Oh, everyone, of course!'

'Well everyone ought to, then.'

'Everyone ought to what?' asked Jessie, suddenly appearing through the doorflaps, with Nathan just behind.

'Know what entomology means,' answered Paul. 'I'm starting up a group for anyone interested in insects...'

'Is anyone interested in insects?' frowned Nathan.

'Lots, for your information! I'm designing posters on my computer, and I was thinking of having badges shaped like tarantulas. What do you think?'

'Oh, cosmic!' chortled Sam. 'Tarantulas? Can't wait to see them!'

'OK! Just because you're terrified of money spiders!'

'Am not!' Sam leapt up and attempted to pummel Paul's chest. His long arms held her away with ease, so she started hitting out at those instead. They'd been mock-fighting for years, with never even a bruise to show for it. Nathan and Jessie ignored them.

'What happened to you at lunch-time?' he asked her, suddenly remembering he'd not seen her at band practice. 'We really needed you. I thought you said you'd be there.'

Jessie's hand shot over her mouth. 'The concert! I completely forgot! Ooh, sorry! My mum's always saying I'd lose my head if it wasn't screwed on!'

'Even Sam showed up, much to everyone's amazement. Maybe you just preferred lazing around in the sunshine?'

'Did not!' she protested. 'I simply forgot. Everyone's allowed to forget things sometimes!'

'Can't argue with that one, can you, Nathan?' teased Sam, stopping her 'fight' with Paul. 'Your memory's even worse than mine!'

'All right! But this is really important to me, you know. My mum says she's going to try to come to the concert, and I want her to be impressed. I want her to see I can be part of something good. And it won't be good at all if people don't bother turning up!'

'I'm sorry. I really did mean to come today.' Jessie immediately felt really bad about forgetting. She knew how hard it was for Nathan at home. His sister wasn't very kind to him, and his mum never seemed to have much time for him, what with her new job taking up even more hours than the last one had, and having his gran to look after as well. If she actually planned to be at the concert, it would be a first! 'I'll be there tomorrow,' she said. 'I promise.'

However, she left the house next day without her instrument, and only remembered when she was nearly at the school gates. 'Oh well,' she thought to herself, 'I can't be bothered to go back for it now. And I don't suppose it matters. I'm sure they can manage perfectly well without me.'

Out in the vineyard, the sun was bearing down hotter than ever. Joash carried what felt like the hundredth basketful of grapes over towards the large cart that would, at the end of the day, be trundled back to the vats near the house, where the grapes would be trodden to squeeze out the juice.

'Expect I'll be asked to help with that, too!' he muttered wryly to himself, as he lifted the basket up over the edge of the cart.

'What's that? Talking to yourself, Joash?' It was Thomas, Abner's uncle, and Joash turned quickly to find the man grinning broadly at him. 'Thought that nephew of mine might have been here with you today. We could have done with his help.'

Joash shrugged. 'He preferred to do something else.'

'And you didn't?'

'Yes, I did, but I—well...' Joash stopped, confused. He was good with fish, but not too good with words!

'You mean you thought it was time you helped your father for a change?' The man took a step or two closer, looking him straight in the eye. 'But you weren't going to first of all, were you, Joash?'

'My friends were expecting me...' Joash said lamely.

'Ah, of course, your friends! Well, good that you changed your mind. You've worked well!' Thomas gave him a friendly clap on the back. 'We're stopping for something to eat now, so sit yourself down and we'll join you in a few moments.'

Thomas tipped the rest of his grapes into the cart, then strode off towards Amos. Joash sank down gratefully on to the ground, glad of the shade provided by the large sheet of goat's-hair tenting, which was spread high over where the cart stood. He stared up at the differently shaded pieces, sewn strongly together, and had a vivid picture of his mother weaving all the goats' hair, many years before, making the pieces for this tenting. He remembered Nahash—probably only about eight—crawling under the half-made tent and hiding, until their mother came in to begin sewing more pieces together. He'd waited a few moments then leapt out with a yell, so that she yelled back in surprise, and they all three fell about laughing. They'd laughed a lot when she'd been alive.

'But where is that brother of mine now, I'd like to know?' he said to himself.

Which was just the same thing Amos was thinking! He could, of course, try to find him again. There was no doubting Nahash knew how much he was needed. However, if he still chose not to come, Amos wasn't going to force him. He walked towards Joash.

'Good news!' he called. 'Word has come from the village that we can expect three of the women to help this afternoon.'

'Does that mean we'll finish the job today?'

'By sunset, certainly,' Amos grunted, as he lowered his chubby body on to the ground beside his son. 'Sorry about the fishing. Another day.'

'Yes. Sorry I was a bit reluctant to...' Joash's voice tailed off as he noticed the struggle of workers making their way over towards them. The men he recognized, of course, but there was a girl—a remarkably pretty girl—walking between them and carrying a basket on her head. 'Er—who's that?' he asked, as carelessly as he could.

'Mmm? Oh, that's Jerusha, Abner's sister. Don't you recognize her? She's been bringing food up for us at noon-time for the past year or so. Of course,' he cast a sly smile in his son's direction, 'if you were out here more often, you'd have known that!'

Joash got to his feet as nonchalantly as he could. 'Abner mentioned his sister might be here, but the last time I saw her she was plain, and…' He positioned his hand at about the level of his waist.

'Ah, well,' grinned Amos, 'you all have this tendency to grow! And some grow prettier than others, wouldn't you say?'

But Joash didn't answer. He was finding difficulty with words, again!

That day was a surprisingly good one for Joash. He discovered that it wasn't so dreadful, after all, spending hours collecting in the grapes. The whole atmosphere in the vineyard had been remarkably cheerful and he'd found it, in fact, very good to be working with his father. And if Jerusha was regularly going to be there he might even consider helping out more often himself!

At sunset, with the crop all safely in the vats ready to be trodden the next day, Amos and Joash walked back into the house, laughing and joking together like they hadn't done since before Joash's mother had died. To celebrate the day, Amos went to get a jug of some of his finest wine, while Joash lit the lamps inside the house. When the light filled the room the first thing he saw was his brother, fast asleep in a corner.

'Hey, lazy bones!' he said, shaking him awake. 'What happened to you, then?'

Nahash leapt up, startled out of his deep sleep, and not really too sure what was happening. 'I'll be right there! Oh, Joash, it's you.' He rubbed his eyes and yawned, 'How did the fishing go? You back already?'

'No, I'm on a boat in the middle of the Sea of Galilee, what do you think! I've been out in the vineyard all day, if you must know—like you should've been.'

'Oh, yes, well, I sort of forgot.'

'Sort of decided not to bother, you mean.'

'No! Just knew you'd be managing perfectly well without me, that's all.'

'We weren't—and you missed a good day, Nahash,' said his father quietly, entering the house. 'A very good day.'

The concert, in the end, went superbly. Even the saxophones no longer sounded like vintage car horns!

'Shame your mum didn't make it,' Sam's dad said to Nathan afterwards. 'She'd have been proud of you.'

Nathan went red and looked at his feet.

'Was your sister here?' prompted Sam's mum. 'I didn't notice her, but there were so many people in there—the place was heaving!'

Nathan shook his head, wishing she hadn't asked. He was so disappointed his mum hadn't shown up. Fortunately Sam appeared at that moment, a broad grin spreading across her freckled face. 'So what did you think of that?' she cried, bear-hugging her dad.

'Excellent!'

'What did my rotten brothers think? Impressed, I bet!' Sam swaggered out into the warm evening air, followed by the others.

'Certainly were,' he agreed. 'They had to slip out after you'd done your solo, but they said to tell you Mr Pettifer is right. You are a strong player!'

'I'll take that as a compliment, then!' she declared. 'So they didn't hear the song that's going to make us famous? Their loss!'

'Was that the new one—the one you did last of all—that some of the children sang along with?' her mum asked Nathan.

'Oh, yes, yes, that's right,' he answered, grateful to have something to be enthusiastic about. 'Mr Pettifer wrote it, and he told us…'

'... only this evening—just before the concert started...' interrupted Sam.

'That's right—only then,' he continued, 'he told us he's going to get us to record it and send it in to...'

'... "Take a Note",' interrupted Sam again. 'You know, Mum, that programme at 4.30 on Tuesdays I always watch.'

'It's a competition,' added Nathan. 'If our school wins we'll get to be on the TV!'

They both started to sing the song, joined by three or four others from the school who were heading down the same road. By the time they reached Nathan's front gate only the title—A.S.L.T.W.—was still recognizable. A zany alternative version of the words had quickly been thought up and Sam's mum was walking along with tears streaming down her face.

Nathan glanced back, worried, and whispered to Sam, 'Is your mum OK? I think she's crying!'

Sam punched him lightly on the arm. 'Don't be daft! She's laughing!'

'Oh! Right.' He walked up to his front door and rang the bell. 'See you tomorrow,' he called as the others carried on down the road.

The door was finally opened by his sister, Denise, and he stepped inside, walking straight through to the kitchen. His mum was sitting at the table peeling potatoes. He looked at her tired, drawn face. He couldn't remember the last time he'd seen her smile, let alone laugh.

'Oh, Nathan—thought you'd never get home! Put the kettle on for me, there's a good boy. I'm longing for a cup of tea.'

He went across to the sink and turned on the tap. 'The concert went well,' he said quietly. 'Wish you'd been there, Mum.'

'I know. I'll try to make it next time. Promise,' she said.

The following week, after school, when everywhere was quiet, Mr Pettifer gathered the band together for the recording. 'Do your best, everyone,' he beamed, 'and we might even get to be famous for fifteen minutes!'

Which was exactly what they were! To everyone's delight, the song won, and the band were invited to perform it on television during the summer holidays. Sam's dad drove her, Nathan and a couple of others up to the studios early one morning, with Sam trying hard to act cool, confident, and in control.

'Boy, am I glad I changed my mind and joined the band!' she said, wriggling round in the back of the car with excitement. 'I bet Jessie's sorry now she never came along.'

And she was, especially when, later that day, she and Paul watched the programme together round at his house. Afterwards, they went out to the Clubhouse.

'It's not fair!' she grumbled, climbing up the ladder behind him. 'I've always wanted to be on TV! Why didn't Mr Pettifer tell us about that bit, when he asked us to join the band?'

'Would it have made any difference? I mean, would you have believed his song would win?' asked Paul, passing her a bag of crisps. 'I certainly wouldn't have. Not with that daft title. I ask you! A.S.L.T.W!'

'Mmm,' Jessie nodded, and didn't like to admit that, when she'd heard the song at the concert, some uncomfortable bells started ringing. Only three weeks before, in Pathfinders at church, they'd been looking at the parable in Matthew 21 that Jesus had told about a man who owned a vineyard, and his two sons. The person leading the group had given the parable his own title, which, oddly enough, had been the same as the full version of Mr Pettifer's song: 'Actions Speak Louder Than Words'.

'You see,' he'd pointed out, having got them to read verses 28 to 32, 'Jesus is showing us that doing the right thing in the end is better than knowing what is the right thing to do, and yet not doing it at all.'

Jessie had an uncomfortable feeling that someone, somewhere, was trying to tell her something!

Bare Cupboards

Nathan, carrying a box so big he could hardly see over the top of it, struggled up the narrow side steps on to the school stage, tripped and fell headlong. Flat on his stomach, he watched with resignation as the box slithered on its side, spilling ancient-looking Christmas decorations in all directions.

'Nicely done!' Paul chuckled admiringly, catching a red bauble as it toppled over the edge, and pushing another box deftly on to the stage.

'I hate Christmas!' Nathan grumbled as he inspected the damage to his trousers. A bit of skin was peeping through the knee. 'Look at that! My mum'll be steaming when she sees. Do you think Jessie'll sew it up for me at lunch-time?'

'Not if she's got any sense! It's about time you learnt to do your own darning.'

'Yeah—that's what my mum says.' Nathan looked even more morose.

Paul hoisted himself easily up on the stage and started collecting together the decorations. 'Anyway, what's wrong with Christmas all of a sudden? I'm getting some new computer games and a racing bike this year. Can't wait!'

'Oh, well—I'll get some great things, too, 'course I will,' Nathan mumbled, not wanting to admit to his mum's comments on the subject only that morning, when she'd made it very clear there would be no money for presents that year. Anyway, that wasn't what was really depressing him.

'Why so miserable, then?' asked Paul, starting to hang decorations on the tree.

'Well, Mum told me a couple of weeks ago that Dad's got to go to Ireland again, and he'll be away all over Christmas. I hoped I might at least have seen him before he left, but I haven't heard from him, so I guess he must have gone already.'

'That's a bit rough. You hardly ever see him as it is. Got any tinsel in there?'

Nathan started to rummage about in the box just as Miss Grant entered the hall. 'Thank you, boys, but the caretaker will hang the decorations, as well you know!' She waved them to get down from the stage and followed them out of the hall, stopping Nathan at the door. 'The Head wants to see you in his office,' she said quietly. 'Go along there now quickly, then come straight back to class.'

Nathan looked up horrified. 'Don't worry!' she said with a smile. 'I don't think it's anything dreadful.'

So Nathan headed off towards Mr Riggs' office, wracking his brain to remember what it was he might have done wrong now! The only thing he could think of was last Thursday lunch-time, when he'd tripped and dropped a plateful of food in such a spectacular fashion that the sausages whizzed back towards the kitchen, the chips flew in every possible direction, and some of the baked beans could still be seen sticking to the hall ceiling! But he'd already been told off for that. By the time he reached the Head's door he was quite horribly certain he must have done something else dreadful without even knowing! He knocked nervously on the door.

'Come in!' Mr Riggs' voice at least didn't sound too thunderous! 'Ah, Norstadt. Good. I've just had the letter we were expecting from your father, which I'm getting a reply off to, and I just wanted you to take a copy of that home for your mother.' He frowned at Nathan's blank expression. 'The letter about you having time off to visit your father next week. He seemed to think you knew.'

'I did? I am?' Nathan stared at the Head, feeling a bit idiotic. He knew he forgot a lot of things, but he surely couldn't have forgotten something as brilliant as that! 'When am I going? I mean—I can't remember.'

The Headmaster sighed. These children and their memories! 'You'll have next Friday off school, then...' he referred back to the letter he'd received, 'you'll be back home on the Sunday evening.' He picked up an envelope and handed it to Nathan. 'Make sure your mother gets this.'

Nathan mumbled his thanks and scurried out of the office feeling light-headed. He was going to see his dad after all. Mega-brilliant!

The rest of the day swept by in a haze. He raced home, and rushed in through the door calling loudly to his mum. She popped her head over the banisters and hissed, 'Stop shouting, Nathan! You'll disturb your gran and I've only just got her settled down after her tea.'

'Sorry!' He leapt halfway up the stairs. 'It's just that Dad wrote to school to ask if I can have Friday off next week, so I can see him before he goes to Ireland.' He waved the Head's letter and looked anxiously at his mum as she came down the stairs towards him. 'Mr Riggs says it's OK. So can I?'

'Of course you can! He phoned about it last week. I'm sure I must have told you. Really, Nathan, your memory!' His mother stepped past him, taking the envelope and disappearing into the kitchen.

'Yes!' Nathan punched one hand into the air in glee. 'Three days isn't long but, "quality, not quantity"—that's what Dad always says!' Maybe Christmas wouldn't be so bad, after all!

The time seemed to drag by, but at last Friday morning came. Nathan was in high spirits but, in the middle of struggling to zip up his holdall, he suddenly stopped and gave a loud groan.

'What's the matter with you?' Denise was just passing and put her head round his door. 'Don't tell me you're getting sick! Dad won't want you around if you're ill, you know.'

'I'm not ill—I've just thought of something.'

'Oh—brain ache! Well, that's not surprising!'

'All the stuff for the school Christmas sale's supposed to be in by today,' he wailed, ignoring her usual sarcasm, and scrabbling under his bed for where he remembered shoving the black plastic bag full of things his mum had collected. He hadn't dared mention to her that they'd specially been asked for reasonably good-quality items (not, Paul joked, the normal rubbish) because he knew she'd only say they didn't have any good stuff. Consequently, he hadn't taken the bag in earlier, hoping he'd be able to include some better bits (he hadn't!) He tugged at it hastily, forgetting how much the old springs of his bed hung down at odd angles.

'You'll tear it, pulling like that!' predicted Denise infuriatingly (because she was right!) and disappeared downstairs.

Nathan sat back on his haunches and stared dejectedly at the bag, now lying beside his bed, with a large hole where a large hole wasn't supposed to be! 'Hall cupboard,' he muttered to himself, dragging the damaged bag and its contents out of his room, and pulling open the door of the large storage space next to the bathroom. It was full to bursting with things that once had been in the front room until it had been turned into his gran's bedroom, but he could just see the end of a roll of black plastic bags sticking out over the edge of the topmost shelf.

'And the star player of the Harlem Globetrotters scores another brilliant goal!' he whooped, leaping up to grab the bags. He pulled them down triumphantly, but in the process also pulled down a box full of all manner of bits and pieces, which toppled on to his head, scattering its contents across the floor.

'Terrific!' he groaned. At that moment a car's hooter sounded from the road outside.

'That'll be your dad!' his mum called up the stairs. 'Aren't you ready yet?'

'Nearly!' Nathan pulled open a new bag, pushed the old one and its contents inside, shoved the scattered items back in their box as quickly as he could, then pushed it back on to the top shelf. He raced downstairs and out of the front door, pausing just to call to his dad, talking to Denise beside the car, that he'd be back in a minute.

He quickly reached Jessie's house, only a few doors down the road, and breathed a sigh of relief at seeing she hadn't yet left for school. 'Here!' He thrust the bag at her. 'Sale stuff! Got to go, my dad's waiting. See you Monday!'

Barak was a shopkeeper.

He'd wanted to be a shopkeeper ever since the day his parents had taken him, aged nine, all the way from Nazareth down into Jerusalem, for his first ever look at the amazing number of stalls and shops the city offered. He couldn't have said what he'd actually put in his shop if he ever got one, but there were plenty of years to think about that! He'd play endless games with his older brothers and sister outside their sun-bleached, wooden-shuttered house, where they'd have to bring small stones to his 'shop' to buy other, bigger, stones.

'What're you selling today?' one of his brothers would ask, "cos I only want a pomegranate!'

'Can't you see it's a meat stall!' Barak would reply scathingly. 'It's obvious it's a meat stall!'

Then other times he'd insist his mother chose from his wonderful selection of 'fine silks'. 'So beautiful, I can hardly see them!' she'd tease, holding a piece of 'cloth' up in the air admiringly.

On a day they would remember years later, little Amos, one of his cousins, ran over from his house to join in the game. 'Want grapes!' he announced, stamping his foot.

'You always want grapes!' Barak sighed.

'Want to squash them!' Amos stamped his small feet up and down on the ground again, demonstrating enthusiastically.

'You'll have to go and work in a vineyard when you grow up, then!' Hashem, Barak's father, laughed, and little Amos gazed up at him and nodded his head solemnly.

This game went on intermittently for some years, without Barak ever managing to make up his mind which thing he liked selling best. Then one day Hashem again took his family down to Jerusalem. This time, though, he didn't stop to wander slowly along the maze of streets, with their strange mixture of smells of perfume, herbs, vegetables and cooked meats. 'I want you all to see something much more important today!' he said, leading them quickly forward.

Suddenly it seemed to Barak they'd stepped out of one world into a completely different other. The first one had been bustling, noisy, and shadily closed in. This other world was spacious and comparatively quiet. The sky above was open and blue, with the sun blazing down. But what really took his breath away was a huge structure towering before him, behind protective walls, like a glistening mountain! It was so golden in colour that he was dazzled, and had to screw up his eyes against the brightness. He never forgot that moment.

'It's gold!' he gasped. 'Is it real gold?'

'Of course!' his father nodded, with pride in his voice.

'Some of the walls are covered with gold, and some with silver, and the rest are made out of the purest white marble.' He smiled broadly and turned to his wife. 'King Herod builds an impressive temple, don't you think?'

'Did he do it all himself?' asked Barak, following his father through the covered cloister that ran round the outer courtyards.

'No!' laughed Hashem. 'He just gives the orders! So they say, there are solid gold lamps and bowls too, which the priests use, all inlaid with jewels—of the most exquisite quality and colour.'

'Is that really true?' asked his wife.

'I don't know,' admitted Hashem. 'Such things are kept in the Priests' Court. But let's go further in and find what wonders we can see.'

He led his family through the South Gate into the Court of the Gentiles, then into the Court of the Women (which was as far as his wife and daughter were allowed to go), then he and his sons went further into the impressive Court of Israel. Here, too, the walls were covered with gold plating. By this time Barak was almost speechless with wonder and, even on the long cart-journey home, while his brothers and sister chattered about all they'd seen (especially the spikes of gold on the roof to keep the birds away, which they thought the best!) he hardly said a word. This was most unusual. A silent Barak was something his mother often longed for. Now she'd got it, she began to worry!

'I can't believe I'm saying this, but you're too quiet!' she exclaimed eventually.

'Oh, sorry! I was just thinking…'

'Ah, that's it, then!' interrupted his sister. 'Thinking! Too much of a shock for your head!'

'Shh!' their mother scolded. 'What were you thinking?'

'I was thinking that if I sold gold and jewels in the shop I'm going to get one day, some of them might go into the temple—mightn't they, Father?' he asked, peering through the dark at Hashem, who would have laughed at the suggestion but for a sharp and painful prod from his wife's elbow!

'Well, I suppose that could happen, yes,' he agreed. 'But

it would take an awful lot of money to fill a shop with things like that, I'm afraid.'

And it had! Barak spent many, many years doing whatever paid the best, in order to save enough to buy his own premises. And then spent every shekel he had left on jewels. The shop wasn't in Jerusalem, but he had a fine spot on the main street in Nazareth, and he was very proud of it.

By the time he managed to achieve this he was definitely not a young man any more. But, on the day he first opened for business, he was a very happy one! He remembered that day well. His cousin Amos, no longer so young himself, had come across from his vineyard (who would have believed his little cousin would have managed to buy the vineyard he'd gone to work in as a young lad!) to help celebrate the occasion.

Barak had just served his first two customers (a bead chain made up of semi-precious stones, and a ruby, to be set by the goldsmith next door into a gold ring) when Amos arrived on his cart, bringing with him a leather bottle full of his best wine.

'Cousin—Shalom!' Barak hugged him boisterously. 'Did you see that? Two sales already!' He folded his rather long, thin body down on to the bench by the shop opening, and indicated for Amos to join him.

'Good, good! It's a fine place you have here, and no mistake! You were always trying to sell us stones when we were children, and now you're doing it for real!' Amos chuckled, mopping his brow, for the heat in the town seemed intense. 'Though how you stand living in this place I can't imagine. Give me my open fields any day!'

'Who's looking after them right now?' asked Barak, standing up as another potential customer approached his stall.

'Joash is in charge. And I really think he quite enjoys it these days—though that probably has more to do with a certain young woman from the village working the vines, than the vineyard itself!'

Barak made his third ever sale, and the two men spent the rest of the day, between the occasional customers, chatting amicably about childhood memories, and their continuing plans for the future.

But all that had been ten years ago. Now there were no less than three other jewel merchants in the town, so competition was hot! It wasn't enough to have a simple, plain stall. Nowadays, it was about who could decorate their shop the most impressively, and who could get the better sales deals.

Eunice, his wife, was talking to him sharply about it at the end of a particularly bad day. 'I'm trying to attract more business!' he replied patiently. 'Didn't I get in all those cheaper jewels, and lower the prices?'

'So you fill the shop with any old rubbish!' she scolded.

'How about my special offer this week? A free silver nose-ring with every two jewels purchased! The young women greatly favour these nose-rings nowadays, you know.'

'Another thing we have the Egyptians to thank for, I suppose!' sniffed his wife, whose nose, Barak couldn't help thinking, was large enough to display several rings rather effectively, though he supposed in her present mood he'd better not suggest it!

But it was certainly a problem. Then early one morning, just as the first cock was beginning to crow, Barak suddenly sat bolt upright on the wool-filled mattress that served as his

bed, a picture before him of just exactly what his shop should look like. It was so clear that, completely forgetting his wife snoring beside him, he shouted out, 'That's it! Of course!'

'What?' she mumbled, suddenly more awake than she cared to be. 'What are you shouting about?'

'I have the answer!' Barak turned his thin body round to face her very ample one. 'We must stop filling our shop with so many cheap jewels! Just because the others do, that doesn't mean we have to.' He kissed her large nose affectionately. 'You were quite right, my dear. We must show them it isn't the quantity that's important, but the quality that really counts!'

It was late on the Sunday evening when Nathan got back from his three days away. As a Christmas treat, his dad had taken him to see Shakespeare's *All's Well That Ends Well* the night before, which they'd spent the whole of that afternoon discussing. Somehow he always felt clever and capable when he was with his dad. Not his usual experience! More familiar was the general lack of interest anyone took in him back home, as he went into the kitchen for some hot chocolate. After a few minutes he made his way sleepily up the stairs.

Denise followed him. 'Well,' she remarked, 'you missed some fun and games this weekend, little brother.'

'I'm not little!' he retorted, going into his room, then poking his head back round the door. 'What fun and games?'

'Mum's favourite brooch has gone missing. The gold leafy one with a pearl set in the middle, that Gran gave her. She's practically turned the place upside-down, looking for it.'

'Well I haven't touched it!' Nathan was automatically on the defensive. He always seemed to get blamed for everything that went wrong in that house! 'Didn't know she had a pearl brooch.'

'Knowing you, that's probably true! She kept it in a box in the landing cupboard for safety. Gran wants her to sell it because we need the money and she says it's worth a lot. Mum doesn't want to because she likes it too much, but Gran was fretting—you know how she does—so I said I'd take it to the local jewellers on Saturday. But it wasn't in the box. Mum's really upset.'

'Oh, well, expect it'll turn up. Anyway,' he said, words from Shakespeare's play still ringing enticingly in his ears, 'I will now to bed, sweet Helena, so...' he gave a flourishing sweep of his arm, bowing low, 'farewell until the morrow!' And with that he closed the door firmly in his very surprised sister's face.

Nathan fell asleep as soon as his head touched the pillow, but suddenly, at three-fourteen a.m. exactly, sat bolt upright, staring straight ahead into the darkness, though it wasn't the darkness he saw, but a vision of a box, tumbling off a shelf, spilling its contents on and around a large, black, plastic bag. And, in that moment, he knew without a shadow of doubt exactly what had happened to his mum's precious pearl brooch: he'd given it to the school jumble sale!

'I bet it was the first thing that got bought! he groaned, flopping back down on the bed feeling sick. 'Mum'll never forgive me if I don't get it back. Oh help!'

The very next day, Barak, hanging an 'Away on Essential Business' notice at the front of his shop, prepared to set off early on the long journey down to Jerusalem.

'Surely there are nearer places to go?' grumbled his wife.
'Not for the best quality, my dear!' he assured her.
'But you're too old to be making such a journey!'
'Nonsense!' Barak laughed. 'I'm as fit as I was twenty years ago!' A sudden shout drew their attention to an approaching horse and cart making its way slowly down the busy street. 'Hello, Nahash!' called Barak. 'Bring the cart down here, there's a good lad.' He turned to Eunice. 'There—you see! With Amos's son, I'll be perfectly safe.'

'Huh! The two of you are both as bad as each other!' she scolded. 'You'll probably just get into double the mischief!' She indicated for Nahash to stow in the cart the large pack of food she'd made up for the journey. 'I suppose you want to waste time seeing what's fashionable in Jerusalem in the way of pots these days!' she sniffed.

'Of course he does!' agreed Barak, amiably slapping a now grown-up Nahash on the back. 'His business is going well these days—isn't it, lad? They say you're the finest potter in the district!'

'Oh, well, I don't know... do they really?' Nahash, looking more like his father than ever, grinned broadly.

Barak climbed as nimbly as he could up into the cart, trying to show Eunice how fit he still was. 'We'll be back in three days. Four, at the most!' And, with that, the two men set off slowly down the road, already deep in conversation.

By the end of their second full day in Jerusalem, Barak felt pretty pleased with his purchases. The jewels he'd bought would make his shop look much more impressive. Emptier, but more impressive! However, he still wanted to see one more man who dealt, so he'd been told, in the finest of fine pearls. Dragging Nahash away from a masterly Jerusalem potter, they travelled north towards Tiberias, a town not far from Nazareth, where he'd been told the man traded.

It took quite a time to get there, and it looked an unpromisingly run-down and neglected place when they did. Barak, leaving Nahash asleep in the cart, banged on the door at the front of the house, which was opened by a man whose welcoming grin showed off a mouthful of black teeth. Barak explained his presence, and the man waved him through a curtain into a dark, smelly back room.

'So, they told you of me in Jerusalem, did they?' He sounded pleased that his fame had spread so far. 'Well, they were right. If pearls are what you want, I am indeed your man!'

He lit two small lamps and, on a long, low table, slowly began emptying out, one by one, several leather pouches, within which were folded pieces of fine silk. 'There!' he said grandly, as each square of material opened to reveal tiny pearls at first, then collections of increasingly larger gems. 'You'll find nothing finer in the temple at Jerusalem!'

Barak walked slowly along the row. Never in his entire life had he seen more exquisite pearls. But even those didn't prepare him for the contents of the very last bag, which the merchant revealed only after all the others had been seen.

'And this,' he said, with a toothy grin, 'is my best—my most treasured—piece of all!'

He folded back the cloth and, nestling inside, was just one single pearl. But what a pearl! It was incredibly large, with a glow which emerged right out of its centre, so that it seemed strangely alive. It was the most magnificent thing Barak had ever seen! All the other jewels in his bag paled into insignificance against this one gem. And in that moment he knew without a shadow of doubt he would have to have that pearl. Whatever it took, however much it cost, he would somehow have to make it his own!

Nathan got up late and skipped breakfast, deliberately avoiding his mum and any awkward questions about missing jewellery. He felt a bit guilty, but decided he'd get into less trouble if he handed the brooch back, safe and sound, at the same time as making his confession! He called for Jessie on the way to school, and waited impatiently for her to find her shoes. This wouldn't have been so bad if it hadn't been for her mum, singing painfully off-key, but with great gusto, in the kitchen.

'Sorry,' Jessie apologized as they finally left the house. 'Mum thinks she's Whoopi Goldberg! You've no idea the plans she's got for our church choir!'

'Oh, that's good!' Nathan nodded, not really listening. 'Look, I don't suppose you remember seeing a kind of valuable-looking pearl brooch in the things I gave you for the school sale last week, do you?'

'If I had, I'd have probably bought it myself!' exclaimed Jessie. 'My mum loves pearls. Hang on a minute.' She stopped and turned to look at him. 'Are you saying you put something in the bag that wasn't supposed to go?'

'Not "put"—not exactly "put",' he winced. 'It just sort of—dropped into it from a great height!'

'Nathan, you're hopeless!'

'Yeah, I know! But it shouldn't be too difficult to find out who bought it. Do you think?'

'I'll ask Maddy. She was looking after the jewellery stall.'

By break-time, in fact, he knew exactly who'd bought it. That was the good news! The bad news was that it was Gavin, one of the oldest pupils in the school, who recognized a good thing when he saw it, and had no intention of handing it back for anything other than a very high price!

'How much?' croaked Nathan, appalled, when Gavin mentioned the figure he had in mind.

'Well, it's a pretty nice brooch. You can't expect me to give it away! I could ask three times that, and it'd still be a bargain.'

'But where am I supposed to get that much money from?' wailed Nathan.

'That,' shrugged the older boy, walking away, 'is entirely up to you!'

'It's not fair!' said Sam indignantly when, after school and up in the Clubhouse, all four of them were discussing the problem. 'He probably only paid a fraction of that for it.'

'Fair or not,' observed Paul, 'it's Gavin's brooch now, so he's got the right to demand whatever he wants.' He grinned. 'Besides, he's bigger than you!'

'Bigger than all of us!' said Jessie. 'What are you going to do, Nathan?'

'There's only one thing to do,' he said with unusual determination, opening two large plastic bags in front of him. 'I've got to get it back for Mum, so…' He emptied out the contents into a heap on the floor, '… is there anything here any of you could buy off me—please?'

Paul picked up some books and cassettes. 'But these are all your favourites!' he said in amazement, putting those down and opening a shoe box, 'and the metal soldiers—these were your dad's, weren't they? And your posters… just about everything you have!'

'I don't care!' Nathan said. However much his belongings had meant to him before, they no longer seemed to matter at all in comparison to getting back his mum's precious pearl brooch.

Barak could hardly take his eyes off the dazzling pearl. He'd asked to see it in daylight, so he and the pearl seller were now sitting outside on the flat roof of the house, in the shade provided by the leaves of a tall palm tree.

The merchant had carefully lifted the pearl out of its pouch and placed it in Barak's hand. 'Feel the smoothness! Feel the weight! Who but God could think up such a miracle as creating gems like these from mere pieces of grit! And the oyster this one came from—a monster, I can tell you!'

Barak could believe it! The merchant leaned back against the wall, and closed his eyes. There was no rush. He knew his business well, and could see a successful sale several hundred cubits away.

Barak was, in fact, trying hard to talk himself out of buying the pearl! 'Eunice will not be pleased with me!' he told himself. 'Especially when I tell her I'd have no intention of ever selling it. No indeed! This is a gem to be put on display —treasured for the rest of a man's life!' He winced at the thought of what she'd say to that! He also winced at the probable cost of it. But, then, maybe it wouldn't be as much as he feared. No harm in asking! So he asked.

'That much?' he croaked, when the merchant mentioned a figure that was more than three times what he'd expected.

'It's probably the most lustrous pearl in the world—an exquisite masterpiece of nature!' exclaimed the owner. 'You wouldn't expect me to give it away, would you?!'

'But I'd have to sell almost everything I have to raise that much money!'

'That, my dear friend,' said the man with an innocent smile, placing the pearl carefully back inside its leather pouch, 'is entirely up to you!'

It was early Saturday morning. Nathan sat in the treehouse, peering at Paul's large Tudor-style home, where lights from an elegantly adorned Christmas tree flickered through the sun-lounge windows.

He hadn't done badly at selling his things through the week, but was still a depressing three pounds short. And now his mum knew the truth about what had happened to her brooch! It was all his gran's fault, too! She'd started imagining that some of her things were missing as well, and going on about how they should get the police round to interrogate the neighbours (she liked the thought of that!) In the end there'd been nothing for it but to own up. He wished he'd done it in the first place.

'Why on earth didn't you tell me about this on Monday?' demanded his mother at breakfast. 'I've wasted hours and hours looking for it! How could you, Nathan?'

'Thought I'd be able to get it back really quickly,' he said miserably, 'but the boy at school—the one who bought it— wants an awful lot of money for it, so it's taken me a lot longer. I've nearly got enough now, though, honest!'

'How much money is he asking for it?'

'And where are you getting money from?' Denise asked suspiciously.

'I'm selling things—my own things,' he added quickly, heading for the back door. 'In fact, I've got to go now and sell some more!'

'Wait a minute,' his mum called. 'What sort of things? Nathan! Come back, I haven't finished with you yet!'

But he was gone, and now, stretched out in the treehouse, was determined not to go home again till he'd got the brooch back.

'Which could be another fortnight!' he exclaimed out loud. 'Unless, of course…'

'Unless of course what?'

'Oh, Paul—gosh, you gave me a start! Didn't see you coming!' Nathan sat up as his friend clambered through the canvas opening, still in his pyjamas and dressing-gown.

'Saw you arrive from my window.' He handed Nathan a crunchy cereal bar and opened up another for himself. 'Bet you haven't had any breakfast!'

'Didn't dare stop!' he admitted. 'Mum knows all about the brooch now and I'm still three pounds short. I've got to get it back! I don't suppose you'd buy those soldiers of mine, would you? They're all I've got left. All that's worth anything, that is.'

'Dunno,' grimaced Paul. 'I'll be getting the latest game for my computer at Christmas—the one that teaches you to fly fighter planes. Not sure I'm too bothered about having a set of little metal soldiers!'

'But they're collectors' items,' Nathan pleaded. 'My dad told me to hold on to them because they'll be worth a lot one day. They're all hand-painted, you know.'

'Mmm… three pounds, huh?'

'Yeah—that's all I need!'

'Too cold to argue!' said Paul, heading backwards on his knees out through the canvas. 'It's a deal, but with one condition.'

'What?'

'You buy them back off me for the same amount as soon as you're able, otherwise I reckon you'll get OK with your mum, and then be in trouble with your dad! Deal?' He put out a hand, palm upwards towards Nathan.

'You bet!' said Nathan, bringing his palm down on to his friend's hand. 'Hey, you don't happen to know where he lives, do you?'

'Gavin? No, but I think my dad probably will. They've got a big sheepdog, and bring it here to Dad's surgery for its jabs.

Come up to the house, and I'll ask after breakfast.'

So Nathan sat in the luxurious kitchen, while Paul went to get dressed. His mum was cooking bacon and eggs. It didn't take much to persuade Nathan to have some. The smell was scrumptious! While she was cooking, Nathan found himself telling her about the pearl brooch, and how he'd sold almost everything he had to get it back.

'You know, that reminds me of something,' she said, frowning and breaking an egg into the pan, 'but I can't remember what. Something I read somewhere once.'

Paul came into the kitchen, plonked himself down at the table, and shoved a piece of paper towards Nathan. 'Gavin's address. He doesn't live far away. I'd come with you but Dad's got some gym equipment arriving this morning. Rowing machine, exercise bike, weights and things. Should be great!'

'There you are.' Paul's mother put a plateful of food in front of each of them. 'Get that down you, Nathan. You're far too thin, you know!'

She was just about to make some toast when she suddenly stopped. 'Oh! I've just remembered! Don't go away, Nathan!'

She went quickly out of the kitchen and returned with a thick book, which she put down on the table beside him. 'There!' she said, tapping it with her hand. He looked at her, puzzled. 'You and that brooch!' she exclaimed. 'Knew it reminded me of something. The story of the merchant and the precious pearl. In one of the four gospels, if I remember rightly.'

She started leafing through the pages, suddenly stopping and prodding her finger at a page. Yes! There you are. Matthew 13, verses 45 and 46. "The kingdom of heaven is like what happens when a shop owner is looking for fine pearls. After finding a very valuable one, the owner goes and sells everything in order to buy that pearl." Just like you and your brooch!' She looked pleased with herself. 'Haven't read that since Sunday School. Funny the things you remember.' And with that she went whistling out of the kitchen, completely forgetting the toast. Nathan stared after her. And he thought *his* mum was odd!

One hour later Nathan walked jauntily back down the

road towards his rather tatty late-Victorian home, feeling on top of the world. Safely tucked away in his jacket pocket was his mum's precious pearl brooch. He realized now why she liked it so much. The leaf parts were made of finely woven gold strands, with the pearl, which was much bigger than he'd expected, appearing like a beautiful, delicate raindrop in the centre. And he also knew just how precious it was, because he'd called into the jeweller's shop on the way home. The value put on it quite took his breath away!

'Good thing Gavin doesn't know what he's just sold to me for fifteen pounds!' he chortled.

Later that day the four friends gathered as usual in the Clubhouse to hear all about it.

'Of course,' said Nathan, grinning at Jessie, 'it's all been rather like the parable in Matthew about the shopkeeper and his precious pearl, I think!'

'What?' Jessie's jaw dropped.

'Ha! Didn't expect me to know about that, did you?' he laughed, poking a finger at her.

'He only does 'cos my mum showed him,' Paul said, making a face.

'Anyway, my mum wasn't even mad at me, like I thought she'd be,' Nathan beamed. 'At least, she was mad at me this morning when I said what'd happened to her brooch, but this afternoon, when I gave her it back, and told her all the things I'd sold, she went all quiet. Then she looked in my room—it's really bare now 'cos I even sold my big posters—and then she kissed me!'

'Yuk!' exclaimed Sam. 'If my mum did that to me I'd consider it a punishment!'

'And hugged me,' went on Nathan, grinning. 'Can't remember the last time she did that, either! She said the brooch meant even more to her now, and she'd never sell it, no matter how much it was worth. Boy!' he sighed, clasping his knees to his chest. 'She looked at me, and looked at her pearl brooch, and you should've seen her face! It was—heaven!'

Nahash awoke with a jolt as the cart started moving. He yawned, taking in Barak's stiff back and set expression. 'No good, huh?' he asked. 'Doesn't look the sort of place you'd find valuable gems kept in, I must say.'

'On the contrary, lad, they were the finest! But I have a problem. A serious problem.'

When they finally got back to Nazareth, the 'serious problem' was standing at the doorway to his shop, arms folded, looking impatient. Nahash decided it was a good time for hurried goodbyes!

'I'll give your regards to Joash and my father,' he called, and Barak nodded as he waved and watched the cart disappear up the narrow street. He turned and smiled hopefully at Eunice.

'Well,' she said crisply. 'Having taken all this time, I trust you've found something worth putting in the shop!'

'Just wait till you see!' exclaimed Barak, leading the way inside and unpacking his leather bag, laying the jewels out in front of her. 'Rubies, emeralds, sapphires, as well as some very fine pieces of jasper and carnelian.'

'Well, I can see they're good quality.' She picked one or two up, feeling the weight. 'But is this all?'

'They're the finest pieces! I've also arranged contacts for getting further supplies without having to go all the way to Jerusalem,' he said encouragingly, unwrapping another pouch. 'And what about these pearls? Exquisite, aren't they!'

'I suppose so, but I had expected more of them!'

'Well,' Barak began cautiously, 'I did have more, but then I,' he took a deep breath, 'sold a few again.'

'Sold...?'

'At a profit. Definitely at a profit!'

'But you're supposed to be selling them here!'

'Yes, but you see I found a special pearl in Tiberias that you'll love—you really will. It'll take your breath away, believe me! However, it's rather expensive, and I need to sell things to get it.' He hesitated. 'Quite a lot of things, actually.'

'What sort of things?' she asked suspiciously.

'My own things, of course!'

'You—part with any of your precious belongings? All to buy something you're then going to sell?'

Barak took another deep breath. 'I'm not going to sell it—ever. It's too perfect for that.'

She stared at him. Had he gone completely mad? She concluded he certainly must have done!

The next morning he started gathering together all his belongings—things that a couple of days before he'd have said he couldn't possibly have parted with, but now just didn't seem to matter in comparison to the pearl. Then he began visiting all his friends and relations to see how much he could sell. They all thought he was a bit daft, but happily paid over their shekels!

By the end of the week, though, he was still three pieces of silver short. He looked around his house dejectedly. There wasn't much left to sell! 'Except my purple cloak!' he suddenly exclaimed. 'My neighbour has been after that for years.'

He lifted the lid of a wooden box in the corner of the back room, and pulled out a finely woven piece of purple cloth, with fringes around the edges. It was his favourite item of clothing, brought out only on special occasions, and admired by everyone. It had come all the way from Tyre, and the dye, he always explained proudly, had come from Mediterranean sea snails! He'd felt most wealthy and impressive when he wore it. 'Still,' he told himself, 'why bother about a cloak, when I can have that pearl?' His neighbour heartily agreed, and happily paid out the final bit of money Barak needed.

And so, the next day, with a great deal of joy and delight, he made the journey back to Tiberias to collect the pearl. It was quite late in the evening by the time he returned. Eunice was already asleep, so he left her undisturbed and lit a small lamp in the shop, unwrapping the pearl carefully and laying it on a piece of deep red, silk cloth which sat in a fine gold casket—something he'd deliberately not sold, but saved just for displaying the pearl. He grinned from ear to ear just at the sight of it.

Suddenly he realized that Eunice was standing behind him, gazing over his shoulder. 'Gracious! It's huge!' she breathed. 'Why didn't you tell me it was this beautiful? It's even got colours in it! I've never seen a pearl with colours in it before.'

He nodded, running a finger over its large, smooth, slightly flattened surface. 'It's called a rainbow hue,' he explained. 'Very rare. I shall name the pearl "God's Promise". People will come from far and wide just to see it.'

She nodded, then waved a finger at him severely. 'We must never sell this, Barak. Never! No matter how much we're offered. This is something to be treasured for the rest of our days!'

'I do believe you're right, my dear!' he agreed, smiling. He glanced around the shop. It appeared rather bare now, but he didn't mind in the slightest. When he looked at the pearl he saw a glimpse of heaven and that, for him, was enough.

Help, I'm Falling!

Accident-prone Maddy, Corine (Jessie's older sister) and an embarrassed-looking boy called Phil were doing a sketch in assembly. Phil wore his father's ancient striped dressing-gown (which was why he was embarrassed!) and Maddy wore the all-purpose red and gold robe out of the wardrobe box, which should have been shortened, but hadn't been.

'I am a Pharisee,' announced Maddy proudly, 'a prayerful and completely good person, and I know God must be very pleased with me!' She gazed upwards and swirled the robe around as she moved to centre stage towards a table with a telephone, inevitably tripping up and frowning at anyone who dared giggle.

'And I am a miserable and greedy tax collector!' Phil hung his head and moved to the far side of the stage. 'Nobody likes me, and I'm sure God doesn't, either.'

'Not surprised, in that outfit!' whispered Paul to Nathan, sitting near the front of the stage.

Maddy picked up the phone, dialled an extremely long number, and waited impatiently until 'God', in the guise of Corine, picked up another phone and answered cheerfully, 'God here, what can I do for you?'

'This is your completely wonderful Pharisee!' replied Maddy grandly. 'It's more a case of what can I do for you!'

'Stop blocking my phone lines for a start!' answered 'God', not so cheerfully. 'All you ever do is tell me what a fine and perfect person you are.'

'Well, it's true!'

'That's a matter of opinion! Anyway, it's that tax collector down there I really want to talk to. Bring him to the phone, please.'

'Ah, I understand!' grinned the 'Pharisee'. 'You want to tell him what a bad, useless person he is. Of course!'

'He already thinks that,' replied 'God'. 'I want to tell him how pleased I am with him.'

'Pleased?' the 'Pharisee' spluttered.

'Yes. He's about to tell me how sorry he is for all the things he's done wrong, and how much he needs me. And I shall tell him how much I love him.'

'Who, him?' Maddy swung an arm in Phil's direction,

knocking the phone to the floor. 'But that's ridiculous!'

'And this is boring!' muttered Paul.

'Oh, it's not that bad!' whispered Nathan.

'So how many tax collectors do you know, then? And what's a Pharisee, anyway? This is all ancient stuff—hasn't got a thing to do with us!'

'S'pose not,' Nathan agreed. The sketch went on for a couple of minutes longer, then the assembly was brought to an end.

'At last, they've finished!' Paul got to his feet as everyone started filing out of the hall. 'Glad it's Saturday tomorrow. Can you make it round to the Clubhouse in the morning? Jessie's coming and I've got something great to show you both!'

'Can't.' Nathan sighed. 'Mum's got an extra shift, so she wants me to stay in with Gran. There's no knowing what she'll get up to these days, left on her own!'

Next morning Jessie stood in the middle of Paul's garden, a little boy at her side. 'There, Danny. What do you think of that, then?' She waited to allow her nephew time to be suitably impressed with the Clubhouse.

Danny looked towards the tree and made a face. At the grand old age of seven (just the day before), he wanted to do more exciting things than look at a rotten old treehouse. Not that it was rotten—or old—in fact, it looked pretty good, but he wasn't going to let Jessie know he thought so! She didn't really want him around, anyway. He'd heard her say so to her mum.

He turned his back on the Clubhouse. 'Bet it hasn't got a TV,' he said sulkily, sticking his hands into the pockets of his shorts. 'My friend's got a treehouse with a TV!'

'Don't tell stories, Danny.'

'It's true!' How come no one ever believed him? He kicked at the grass with his trainer.

'Hey, you'll have my dad after you if you do that!' Paul ran over to join them, crouching down and patting Danny's tightly cropped black hair. 'Hi there! You were only five the last time I saw you. Pretty grown-up now, aren't you?'

Danny looked at him sideways, not sure if he was being teased or not. He hated being teased—almost as much as he hated having his head patted! 'I'm seven,' he announced, 'and I want to see my video!'

Paul glanced quizzically at Jessie. 'Mum bought him one for his birthday,' she explained. 'He's seen it three times already, so she made me bring him with me to get him out of the house. Besides,' she grimaced, 'she and my auntie were practising a song they're going to do in church tomorrow...'

'And you didn't want to stay and hear? I am surprised!' teased Paul.

'Got a football?' interrupted Danny. The morning wouldn't be so boring if he could kick a ball around.

'Yes, but you can't play here. My dad would be mad if his plants got damaged.'

'Then where can I play?' asked Danny petulantly. Anyone over seven, it seemed to him, just had no idea how to have fun!

'On the green across the road,' answered Paul. 'But not yet! Your cousin needs to see something on my computer first. Go up into the treehouse and wait for us. We won't be long. Then, if you're very good, we'll have a game. OK?'

Danny didn't answer, just stared appealingly upwards with his large, brown eyes. It's what he did when his mum gave him an answer he didn't like, and then she usually gave him a better one. Maybe it would work with his cousin's friend. It didn't!

'Come on,' said Jessie taking his hand, 'It's a bit high up. I'll help you.'

'Don't need any help.'

'Then I'll undo the rope ties for you! You ought to feel pleased, you know, being allowed in our Clubhouse. No one except our gang goes up there. Hey!' she stopped and called back to Paul. 'I've just thought of something. He could be the gang's mascot. How about it?'

'Brilliant!' laughed Paul.

'Don't want to be a mascot,' retorted Danny, who didn't know what a mascot was.

'That's a shame,' said Jessie, following him up the ladder and undoing the canvas flaps, 'because mascots get their pick of sweets out of the goodie cupboard!' She opened the cupboard door to reveal several plastic boxes containing crisps, popcorn, mini chocolate bars, fruit and raisins. Danny grinned at the sight and she wagged a finger at him. 'Just don't eat too much and don't leave the treehouse!'

'Better not be long,' she said, joining Paul. 'Or he'll eat so much he'll get sick!'

'That's OK. Just want you to see the final draft of my entomology magazine before I print it out.' He led the way through the house. 'Get the benefit of your artistic eye!'

'Oh, yes?' Jessie gave him a sideways look. She knew all he really wanted was admiration for his work. Actually what he did was always good, which was the trouble! Sometimes, in spite of how much she admired him, she couldn't help wishing he'd make a few mistakes, like the rest of them. Then, maybe, he'd be a bit more sympathetic when they got things wrong! Even losing his cockroach, all those months ago, he'd never thought of as his fault.

'Then Nathan can cast his squeamish eye over it…' he continued.

'And Sam can give it her critical eye!' Jessie added.

'Exactly! Except she won't find anything wrong.'

'Have you put in that we have flying cockroaches in Jamaica?' Jessie asked, hoping to tell him something he didn't know. 'Huge ones, so Dad says.'

'Er, not yet! Hey, did I tell you I've got fifteen members in the group now? Pretty good, huh?'

'All with their tarantula badges, I suppose?' she teased, following him into his room and trying not to feel envious. One end of the bedroom was separated off into a raised study area, with a door to his own bathroom. Just the bathroom was bigger than her entire bedroom! He started setting up his computer, and she wandered over to the window, seeing Danny's face peeping out from one of the treehouse lookouts. She waved, but got no response, so turned to watch what Paul was doing.

Danny had seen her, but didn't feel like waving back. He

clambered out on to the Clubhouse platform, stuffing his mouth with crisps. One day he'd get a treehouse like this—only better, of course. He peered over the edge. High up? It was practically on the ground! He looked upwards. The branches spread way above him, so he couldn't even see the sky.

And then a sudden idea came into his head. He'd show them he wasn't a baby any more! He went back through the canvas flaps and over to the largest of the look-outs, which opened out beside the broad trunk of the tree. He wriggled out on to the branch just below and easily pulled himself up to the next, and then the next. He was enjoying himself now. This was much better than watching a video! Soon he was level with the flat roof of the treehouse, so he climbed on to that, feeling like the king of the castle.

Danny would have stayed there and enjoyed giving his cousin a surprise when she came back to find him, except that he suddenly saw a squirrel scampering up the tree above him. He liked squirrels. He began to climb again, to see if he could catch it...

Meanwhile Jessie was having to admit that Paul had made a good job of the mag. It was full of information, pictures, quizzes, all sorts of stuff—even a jokes page. 'What do you get if you cross a centipede with a parrot?' she read out loud.

'A walkie-talkie!' Paul, standing by the window, answered for her. 'Great, isn't it!' It wasn't a question, but she nodded in agreement, anyway.

She went across to join him. 'Better get back to Danny now, and go and play football, I suppose.'

After a minute or two Jessie was climbing up the ladder. 'Hope you haven't stuffed yourself with too much choco...' her voice trailed off, as she saw that the Clubhouse was empty—except for a lot of scattered crisps. For a moment she couldn't think where Danny could be, then had a sudden thought. 'If you've crammed yourself into the goodie cupboard you'll be in trouble!'

'Anything wrong?' Paul's voice wafted up to her from below.

'He's not here!' Jessie flung aside the canvas flaps and

looked anxiously down at him. 'I thought you said he didn't leave. You said you were keeping watch.'

'I was. I did! He never came down the ladder.'

'Then where is he?'

Suddenly a frightened whimper of 'help!' from somewhere up above gave her the answer she didn't want. 'Oh no! He must be up the tree!'

'No problem,' Paul said confidently, reaching up and pulling himself on to the first branch, as she skimmed down the ladder to the ground. 'I'll easily get him down.'

Within just a few moments he was level with the Clubhouse roof. He'd been climbing this tree since he was five. 'Just like a monkey,' his mum always said. 'Just like Superman!' he always thought. There were those in school who thought he was conceited. Well, maybe he was—just a bit! But he'd been brought up believing he was special, so took it for granted he'd be stronger and cleverer than anyone else. He could already see the local rag's headlines: BRAVE YOUNG HERO SINGLE-HANDEDLY RESCUES LITTLE BOY!

'Scared of nothing, that's me!' he called down to Jessie, hanging by one hand and swinging himself up on to the next branch. 'Bet you don't know anyone else who can climb as well as me.'

Actually all Jessie was interested in was Danny getting rescued! She peered upwards, just managing to catch a glimpse of his stripey jumper. 'Paul, please be careful!' she called anxiously. 'He's ever so high up.'

'Don't worry! This is no weakling you see here! I've got my own gym in the house now and spend two whole hours a week just exercising. Are these muscles, or what?' And, with great pride in his abilities, he hauled himself up the branches. 'Bet you ten quid I get him down before you can say, "Paul, you're absolutely brilliant!"'

Zadok lived in the bustling, crowded city of Jerusalem. He was a tailor by trade, something you would immediately have known if you'd seen him walking through the market-place, because at such times he wore a large bone needle in his cloak to advertise his trade. If he'd been a carpenter you would have noticed a wood chip tucked behind his ear, and if you'd wanted a faded robe dyed, you'd have looked for the man sporting a brightly coloured tag of cloth!

In actual fact, Zadok didn't much care for his job, but it did at least pay the bills. However, he was very proud also to be a Pharisee.

Being a Pharisee meant that he was part of a strict religious group of people, whose responsibility was to explain to the ordinary people about the hundreds of laws (covering the smallest detail of everyday life) that the Pharisees had long ago created. They firmly believed that keeping these laws made them more perfect and pleasing to God.

So, when he wasn't making clothes, he was teaching about the laws, and trying very hard to make sure the 'common' people kept every single one of them. Most people failed in this, and he found he didn't have much patience with them.

He would sit in the temple area explaining the intricate rules about exactly how they should wash; what foods they should and shouldn't eat (and how to prepare and cook them so everything was done precisely right); how far away from their villages they were allowed to walk on Saturdays (the day known as the Sabbath), and many, many other confusing and elaborate regulations that left most people's heads spinning! It was a source of great satisfaction and pride to Zadok that, as far as he was aware, he managed to keep every one of the laws!

On this particular Sabbath he was taking a short, early afternoon walk through one of the villages that nestled close to the edge of the city, being very careful, of course, not to walk further than was permitted on this special day of the week. These walks were a habit he'd acquired not long after becoming a Pharisee, because he'd quickly discovered how often he would notice someone who needed just a little reminder about some rule that had obviously slipped their mind. And Zadok was only too happy to help them by giving them that reminder!

He walked slowly, pleased by the silence of no work being carried out. 'Just as it should be,' he said to himself, strolling between the houses that were bunched together untidily around a small, usually hectic, shared courtyard. The area was cluttered with chicken coops, dovecotes, woodsheds and other small storehouses, and the animals in them provided the only noise as he passed through—and a great deal of the smell, though he was so used to that he didn't notice! On every other day of the week the courtyard would have been full of women doing their laundry, or cooking over charcoal fires, while their children played and a wide variety of animals scampered, slept, waddled and wandered.

But now it was peaceful and unusually cool for the time of year, so Zadok quickened his step towards the path leading back towards the city walls, and the temple within, which was where he intended spending the rest of the day. And that was when he saw it! He was helped by the fact that the house he was passing had a broken shutter at one of the narrow windows, so that a sudden unexpected light couldn't help but catch his eye. The moment he glimpsed it, he stopped in his tracks, turned, and strode over to the small, mud-brick building, pushing open the wooden door without bothering to knock. What he saw astonished him!

'What do you think you're doing?' he demanded severely of a young girl—probably not more than sixteen years old—who was kneeling down beside a small fire in the middle of the single room that was her home. Unusually, she was alone, because the other five members of her family (her husband, his mother and grandmother, and two unmarried sisters), who all shared the small living space, were in other houses at that moment, or still at the temple.

Sarah gasped and scrambled to her feet, almost catching the hem of her robe in the flames. 'Light—lighting a fire!' she stammered, confused by this imposing stranger bursting in on her. She didn't recognize him, but instinctively knew from his air of authority that he must be one of the Pharisees.

'I can see that!' exclaimed Zadok. 'What I want to know is, what are you doing lighting a fire today?'

'My son…' she took a nervous step towards a baby, crying fretfully in its wooden cradle. 'My son is very ill. I need warm water for him and…'

'But it is the Sabbath!' interrupted Zadok in amazement. 'As you couldn't possibly fail to know, any kind of work is against the law on the Sabbath, and, specifically, lighting fires in homes is against the law on the Sabbath!'

'Yes, but—my son is very sick,' she whispered, biting her lips to keep back the tears. 'I thought God would understand…'

Zadok, however, didn't agree at all, and insisted she put the fire out immediately. 'You must not light it again until after the Sabbath is over,' he instructed severely, turning on his heel and leaving the house. As he walked away he felt very confident that he'd done exactly what God had wanted him to do. The girl only had a few hours to go without a fire, and breaking the law would, quite clearly, have been far, far worse! It was just as well he'd been passing by really, he thought to himself. He would personally pray for the baby, which would do it a great deal more good than any fire, of that he had no doubts at all.

On his way to the temple, making sure he wouldn't walk one single step beyond the permitted one kilometre, Zadok went over in his mind the reasons for the myriad of Pharisee laws. It was true that there were rather a lot of them, and the ordinary people found it difficult to remember, let alone manage to keep them, but it was also perfectly clear that they were there to protect the people. After all, if these hundreds of other rules were kept, it would be quite impossible for anyone to break any of God's actual laws. It made perfect sense to Zadok.

Once inside the temple, and standing away from the rest of the men there (making it clear to everyone that he was a Pharisee), he began his long, involved prayers, not forgetting to make his request for the child's recovery. He was certain God would answer this particular prayer, considering who was making the request! Gazing upwards at the golden ceiling, he smiled to himself and prayed, 'God, I thank you that I have been chosen to keep your laws, and all those laws which reinforce yours. I thank you that I've always known I was special—that you made me good enough to help rescue your people from falling.'

He glanced out of the corner of his eye across at the other men, trusting that his lengthy prayers were duly noticed and appreciated—one needed to set a good example, after all! 'I thank you, Lord,' he went on, 'that I'm not greedy, dishonest and unfaithful like so many others, who don't go without eating for two whole days a week, as I do, or give you one tenth of all the money they earn, as I always do!' The thought of money, which he never had much of, brought his notice to another man, standing away from everyone else, in a corner of the temple. He recognized him as one of the most hated of all the country's citizens. Gazing upwards again he continued fervently, 'And I'm really grateful to you, Lord, that I'm not like that wicked tax collector over there!'

When he eventually finished his prayers and left the temple, it was just as the ram's horn was being blown, telling everyone in the area that the Sabbath was over. Zadok headed for home, feeling pretty pleased with himself, and quite convinced that God was, too.

Jessie had been relieved to see Paul disappear up the tree so fast. She was the first to admit she was no good at climbing. It was all she could do to get up the climbing bars in the school gym, and had never liked to admit that even getting down the ladder from the Clubhouse often made her feel dizzy! She didn't think there was any way she would have been capable of trying to save her little cousin herself.

'Hold on tight, Danny!' she called out. 'Paul's coming for you. You'll be safe soon!' She tried to sound as calm as possible, but really she was horribly frightened. He'd climbed so high! She couldn't bring herself to look up again to see how far Paul had reached, but could hear Danny crying out for help. She buried her face in her hands and called out anxiously, 'Are you nearly there yet, Paul?'

'Well, I can see him.' Paul's confident-sounding voice floated down to her. 'He's stuck on some thinner branches a bit further up.' Muffled tones told her he was probably talking quietly and reassuringly to Danny, but the mention of thin branches didn't reassure her much!

She felt useless. 'Why aren't I as good as Paul?' she muttered out loud. 'And why did I have to be so annoyed about looking after Danny? He isn't that much of a nuisance! I should've taken care of him properly, instead of just thinking about what I wanted to do.'

Only the previous Sunday, in the short talk before she and the rest of the children's groups went out of church and into Sunday Club, they were being asked to try to care about each other's needs, rather than just their own. 'Think about how you want to be treated,' the person giving the talk had said, 'then see if you can be like that to your friends. It's not easy,

I know! I've got an elderly neighbour who lets the weeds in his garden grow practically up to his chin, and it does annoy me so, because they spread into my garden and it's jolly hard work to get rid of them. I was complaining about it to someone a few days ago, but, instead of sympathizing with me, they said I ought to make the time to help him keep his garden in order. And then I felt awful, because they were quite right. It's what I'd want my neighbours to do, if I was too old to look after things myself.'

Jessie had thought at the time that it had been a bit of a silly example. None of them cared very much about weeds, chin-high or otherwise! But now she was beginning to get the point. 'If I hadn't been so selfish,' she said angrily to herself, 'Danny would have been all right! If I'd thought about what he needed, I wouldn't have left him all on his own, and he wouldn't now be in danger.' But he was in danger, and she felt so useless. Then, quite suddenly, she realized there actually was something she could do to help!

'Paul!' she yelled. 'Is that big ladder still in your garage?'

'Should be.' His voice, sounding a little distant now, wafted down to her. 'But you don't have to bother. I've nearly got him!'

However, another loud wail from Danny sent Jessie chasing back down the garden towards Paul's house. 'I'm going to get the ladder,' she called, 'and your mum, if she's still in!' As she ran she prayed hard. 'Please, Jesus, don't let Danny fall. I'm so sorry I didn't look after him properly. Let him be safe, and I promise I won't be selfish ever again! Please help Paul, and please, please, please don't let Danny fall!'

The overweight, wealthy tax collector, so despised by Zadok (and everyone else he met) was the sort of mean man who, if he'd gone into Barak's shop (and if Barak had still had anything in his 'Cheap and Cheaper Still' cupboard), would have been more interested in those goods than in anything else, even though he could easily have afforded to buy the best.

He was well aware he wasn't the city's most popular man and usually that didn't bother him. He was proud that the Roman government employed him to do a difficult job, and he did it well. True, he charged the people a little bit extra here and there—well, actually quite a lot!—which he kept for himself, but saw no reason why he shouldn't.

However, on this particular Sabbath day, hiding himself away in a corner of the temple, he was beginning to have serious doubts about his life. And all because of his nephew!

It had started when his youngest sister, her baby son wrapped up tightly in her arms, had stood at his doorway several days earlier, shrilly demanding, 'Why can't you get the potions for him, Azarel? It isn't far to Eizariya!'

'Must you always speak so loudly?' he'd demanded, quickly pulling her inside. 'I have my job to do. I can't just take off at a moment's notice! It's your husband who should go, instead of staying on that boat of his. Anyway, surely the Jerusalem women have medicines?'

'I've tried all those but the baby's still sick. There's a woman in Eizariya who grows special herbs. I'm certain she could help. Please go to her for me.' She'd looked at him pleadingly, tears beginning to well up in her eyes.

'Oh, don't! You know I can't stand it when you cry!' Striding back towards the door, Azarel had pulled it open, saying, 'I'll go, all right?' He'd raised one hand quickly to stop her asking more. 'As soon as I can. That's the best I can offer!'

But there were still taxes to collect, and his private takings to hide away where no one could find them. 'Can't trust anyone these days!' he often complained. And, somehow, he just hadn't found the time to make the journey.

And now it was the Sabbath. He'd had bad dreams all night, and woke up feeling guilty about not helping his sister, and rather worried about the baby. He hadn't dared risk her temper by calling at the house, so went to the temple instead, to say a prayer or two, but didn't stay long—there was a Pharisee there giving him such dark looks!

He hurriedly made his way home and started counting his money. That usually made him feel better! He didn't notice the time drifting by, but suddenly there was his brother-in-law, hammering on his door and insisting he go with him on the journey to Eizariya for medicine for his nephew.

'But I was just about to get something to eat!' he protested. 'And anyway, it's still the Sabbath. It's against the law to travel such a distance.'

'Are you deaf? Didn't you hear the ram's horn being blown from the temple?' Impatiently, he pulled Azarel out of the house towards the animals he'd brought with him. 'I have lanterns. We must go now. The boy is too sick to wait longer.'

And so, with Azarel's large stomach gurgling loudly, they set off for the small village. On the way, his brother-in-law told him how his sister had been scared half to death, earlier that day, by one of Pharisees barging into their house, and forcing her to put out the fire she'd lit for their sick baby.

'A great giant of a man!' he reported. 'Practically broke the door down, so she said. Terrified, she was!'

Azarel nodded sagely. Those Pharisees! Thought they could do anything!

It was dawn when they returned to his sister's house, but by that time he'd made the surprising discovery that it actually felt good to be doing something to help. The baby, lying so still in its cot, really did look very sick indeed. Even with the help of the herbs, though, there wasn't much immediate improvement.

'Go to the temple,' his sister pleaded. 'Make an offering—some money. I'm sure it'll help.'

'Money?' Azarel looked astonished.

'Yes! You have more than enough. Don't tell me you don't!' She felt her temper rise as she pushed him out of the house. 'It's something you can do, so do it!'

And so there he was, back in the temple on the Sunday, making his offering and trying to pray. Going to the temple two days in a row was unheard of for him, and a tax collector giving money away was an amazing sight. The priests and Pharisees certainly noticed!

However, Azarel felt so bad he didn't dare even raise his face towards heaven. He couldn't help noticing that Zadok was having no such trouble! He'd have liked to have asked him to make a special prayer for his sick nephew, but didn't dare. He would have been pretty amazed to know that Zadok was praying for Azarel's nephew at that very moment!

'It's my fault the baby's so ill!' he thought unhappily, burying his face in his hands. 'Why didn't I make that journey sooner? Why did I think only of myself and what I wanted to do? Why did I see the boy only as a nuisance?' He hung his head lower still.

'God, have pity on me,' he prayed. 'I am such a sinner!' He pounded his chest in distress. 'I need your forgiveness, Lord. I've been living so selfishly but, with your help, I promise I'll change. Just please, please, please let my nephew live!'

Hurrying as best they could back up the garden, carrying the long metal ladder between them, Paul's mum and Jessie were hugely relieved that Danny was obviously still managing to cling to the branches of the tree. But they could hear him whimpering, and they both glanced anxiously upwards. What they saw made them gasp. Paul had managed to get closer to Danny, but was now hanging upside-down from a thin branch, which didn't look anywhere near strong enough to take his weight!

'I'm so sorry,' Jessie said as Paul's mum started putting up the ladder. 'It's all my fault!'

Paul twisted his head to look downwards. His confident grin looked a bit lop-sided. 'I've nearly got him,' he called. 'Don't worry!'

'Hang on, both of you!' his mum replied, more calmly than she felt. 'I'm going to get the ladder as close to you, Danny, as I can. Whatever you do, don't move, and you'll be fine!' After a bit of manoeuvring she said, 'The top of the ladder looks quite close, so I'm going up now. Hold the ladder steady for me, Jessie.'

She swiftly climbed up and, within an amazingly few moments, had got Danny on to the top rungs of the ladder.

Persuading him to place one foot below the next, to get himself down the steps, took a little more time, but eventually he made it to the ground, by which time he was grinning like a Cheshire cat and enjoying all the attention! Jessie lifted him high in the air and twirled him around joyfully.

'Don't know why you were so worried!' he laughed. 'I was fine!'

'Sure you were!' she agreed, wiping away both his tears and hers.

It was just at that moment, when Paul's mum was starting to move the ladder to get it closer to him, that they heard an ominous cracking sound and, with a strangled yell, Paul crashed out of the tree, landing in an embarrassed heap on the grass.

'I'd very nearly rescued him!' he groaned, writhing around on the ground and holding his ankle. 'Another minute or two and I'd have been there. Just got stuck on some thin branches, that was all!'

Azarel hurried back towards Sarah's home, anxious to find out how his nephew was, but almost afraid to do so.

It wasn't her temper he was worried about now, though, but the way he'd been living his life. Maybe it hadn't been right to take all that extra money from the people. The other tax collectors did it, but that hadn't meant he'd had to. Sarah always said he'd pay for his greed and selfishness one day, but now he was wondering if the baby was somehow paying for all the things he'd done wrong, instead. He shook his head. No, that just couldn't happen!

He felt depressed and guilty. Sarah's door and all the shutters were ominously closed. 'What if he's worse?' he muttered to himself. 'I daren't go in if he's worse!'

Never the bravest of people, he decided to peep through the broken shutter to see what was happening inside, and was just balancing on a rock to raise himself up high enough when suddenly the shutter was flung open from the inside, sending him sprawling backwards on to the ground! The next thing he knew, Sarah was kneeling beside him and kissing him enthusiastically on his podgy cheeks!

'What in all the heavens were you doing down there?' she asked, helping him to his feet and pushing him towards the open door.

'Praying, of course!' Azarel replied sarcastically, brushing himself down.

'Well, your prayers have been answered!' she laughed. 'Come and see.'

He stepped inside the house, now full of people, one of whom was holding his little nephew, who was obviously well and enjoying all the attention. Azarel was so relieved, he went straight to the baby and, lifting him high into the air, twirled him around with great delight. 'Thank you, Lord!' he shouted.

He then kissed the boy, handed him back and hurried towards the door. 'Are you leaving already?' Sarah asked, surprised.

'I made a promise that if he lived, I would change.' He stopped on the threshold and smiled warmly towards her (which, she thought, was a big change already!) 'I'll make more offerings at the temple, then I'll arrange to make proper provision for my nephew. And I promise you I'll never, ever overcharge people again!'

He walked buoyantly down the road, leaving Sarah watching in amazement. 'Well!' she said, kissing her son. 'You may be only nine months old, but you've done more for my brother in one day than the rest of the family have been able to do in thirty years!'

Meanwhile, back at the temple, Zadok was finishing his prayers. He always had a mental picture of each one of them lifting him higher and higher towards God. And he'd certainly reached some heights that Sunday morning! 'I may not be absolutely perfect,' he told himself as he left the temple. 'Some days it's harder than others, and we all fall sometimes—even me—but not often, of course!'

Paul hobbled into the kitchen. His mum and dad were already sitting, ready to eat a late evening meal, and he winced as he eased himself down on to a chair opposite them. His ankle actually wasn't hurting much now, but he had some pretty impressive bruises appearing on his hip, and there was no point in missing out on a little extra sympathy, he always thought! The town rag's headline had changed in his mind now to: BRAVE LOCAL BOY INJURED IN ATTEMPT TO SAVE SMALL CHILD! He wondered how soon it'd be before a reporter turned up on the doorstep!

He also expected that, any minute, his parents would praise him for his brave attempt at rescuing young Danny. However, his dad didn't say a word but just started dishing up the lasagne they were having.

'Your lasagne, Dad. Great!' Paul said enthusiastically. His parents shared the cooking, but his dad was definitely the best at it. He handed a plateful to his mum, but still neither of them said a word, which Paul found odd.

'So Danny's OK, then?' he said finally, beginning to feel just a little uncomfortable.

'Danny is just fine, Paul,' his dad replied quietly, sitting down. 'But that wasn't any thanks to you, was it?'

Paul frowned. 'Well, I did try to get him down! You should've seen me! I really shot up that tree…'

'Yes, but that wasn't the point, was it? It wasn't about how good you are at climbing trees, Paul.'

'We know you were trying your best,' his mum put in gently.

'But, in this case, your best would have been getting the ladder up to him in the first place. If it hadn't been for Jessie's good sense to go and get help,' his father pointed out, 'we might have been visiting Danny in hospital by now. While you were showing off about how well you think you can climb, that little boy could have fallen and seriously hurt himself!'

'I hurt myself!' Paul protested plaintively. This wasn't going at all how he'd expected it to. He thought his parents would be really pleased with him. They usually were!

Zadok was having a nightmare! Which was strange, because he should have been sleeping contentedly. He'd walked home earlier from the temple, through the area where the baby lived, and found a woman pulling water up from the local well. He went across to her, and asked about the little boy.

'The fisherman's child?' the woman had replied, her eyes widening. 'Yesterday—dying. Today—as healthy as they come! A miracle, that's what it is!'

'Prayers and laws!' he'd corrected, wagging a thin finger at her. 'My prayers on the child's behalf, and ensuring everyone keeps the laws. That's what did it! You tell everybody so.'

He'd left her open-mouthed and suitably impressed, he thought, and had returned home feeling more than pleased with himself. Which was why it was strange that, in his dream, he saw a figure, who he somehow knew was God, standing in the shadows, holding a baby out towards him, demanding, 'What did you think you were doing, Zadok? Why didn't you take care of my son? This child is worth more than all your laws!'

'But, Lord,' he protested, 'the laws are yours!'

'No!' God's voice was sad. 'Love me, each other, and yourselves. Those are my laws. You're so concerned with your own importance, you forget what I've told you. You forget that you need me!'

'But the baby lived!' Zadok exclaimed. 'I prayed for hours and the baby lived. I thought you'd be pleased with me!'

'So you did it all by yourself?' The voice seemed to thunder all around him, filling his head with the sound.

'Yes! No! Not exactly!' He shuffled his feet, no longer sure of anything. Suddenly there was a light all around him so fiercely bright he had to clamp both his hands over his eyes. As he did so, he had a feeling of falling from a great height and, just as he was about to hit the ground, he awoke, finding himself lying on his mattress on the floor of his house, the sun streaming though the window straight down into his eyes.

When Jessie had finally got home with Danny, blurting out to her mum and auntie the whole story—how it had been all her fault, and how terribly sorry she was—they'd fussed around him anxiously, allowing Jessie to escape up to her room. Her father, she knew, was going to be very angry with her when he got home and heard all about it.

She'd heard Danny being put to bed, protesting that it was too early, and later had heard the familiar sound of her dad's motorbike on the driveway. She waited miserably in her room until suddenly there was a knock on the door, and she heard her mum's voice. 'Come downstairs now, Jessie. It's time for supper.'

'I'm not really hungry, Mum.'

'Come down, anyway. Your dad's back and we need to talk to you.'

So, a few moments later, she stood by the kitchen table and, for the second time that day, didn't feel able to raise her head.

'Well, Jessie,' her dad said, 'I think we have to congratulate you.'

She looked up, surprised. Of all the words she'd expected him to say, they certainly weren't those! 'Congratulate?' she

repeated. Was he teasing her? He often did, but surely not at a time like this!

'Why, yes. I spoke to Paul's mother over the phone and understand that, if it hadn't been for your quick thinking and good sense, that pickle of a little boy upstairs could have got himself into serious trouble.'

'He climbed the tree, Dad. He climbed so high! And it was all my fault. I shouldn't have left him. And I prayed and prayed he'd be all right. It was so awful, and I'm really, really sorry.' The words came tumbling out. It was a relief to be able to say them.

Her mum reached out a hand and patted hers. 'From what Danny said, he should've been quite content with all the popcorn and sweets you left him with!' She glanced at her sister, who nodded in agreement.

'Never happier than when he's getting into trouble, that one!' she sighed. 'Worse than my other three put together!'

'Then—you're not mad at me?' Jessie asked, her large brown eyes widening even further. 'I thought you'd never forgive me!'

'You did well, Jessie,' her dad said, smiling. 'You got help, and you've realized where you went wrong. I think you've learnt a big lesson, haven't you?'

'Oh, yes!' Jessie giggled with relief. 'Never, ever, take your eyes off a seven-year-old!'

Azarel was just putting more of his money into the temple boxes when he noticed Zadok leaving. He momentarily wondered where he was going, then quickly shrugged off the thought. Wherever he was off to, it certainly couldn't have anything to do with him, he decided, little knowing that Zadok was at that moment heading towards Sarah's house to make his enquiries about the baby! Taking a deep breath, and gathering up all his courage, he walked across to one of the priests and asked if he could speak to him.

'Of course,' the old man replied quietly, indicating a place they could talk away from the rest of the people. 'Something is troubling you, I can see!'

Azarel then proceeded to tell the priest the story about his nephew, confessing how little he'd cared, at first, about the boy, and how bad he now felt about all the money he'd taken from people through the years.

'I shall make it up to them, though,' he said anxiously. 'I shall give back much more than I ever took, I promise!' Once he started talking about it, it was a real relief, and the words just seemed to tumble out.

'But I'm afraid,' he finished, bowing his head low, 'that God must be very angry with me for the way I've led my life. How can I possibly hope for God to forgive me?'

Much to his amazement, the priest laughed. He didn't know priests were allowed to laugh! He lifted his head and saw the old man's eyes wrinkled up with delight. 'I'm sorry,' the priest apologized. 'I'm not laughing at you. It's just that you look so worried, and you have no need to be. God is already very pleased with you, and forgives you. I can promise you that.'

'How—how do you know?'

'Because,' he smiled, 'you have seen all the things you have done wrong, and are determined to put them right. You asked for God's help, even though that was difficult for you. And you have learnt a very important lesson, I think?'

'Oh, indeed I have!' chortled Azarel. 'Never, ever, underestimate what a little baby can do to change your life!'

Paul wandered into the hall on the Monday morning, still feeling fed up that he'd got into trouble over Danny, whereas Jessie was being treated like a heroine! He was looking for a book Miss Grant said she'd left on the stage, and absentmindedly picked up a piece of paper lying on the floor. He was just about to screw it up to throw in the bin, but glanced at it first. It had obviously been Maddy's 'crib' sheet for Friday's assembly about the Pharisee and tax collector, with most of her words scrawled across it in her messy handwriting. Then, at the bottom, printed clearly, were the instructions:

Read out Luke chapter 18, verse 14. Jesus said: 'If you put yourself above others, you will be put down. But if you humble yourself, you will be honoured.'

'And if you climb too high, you're bound to fall!' Paul added out loud, smiling ruefully. 'Thanks! I think I get the message!'

Sample Drama Script

Hi! Paul speaking. Why not try acting out our stories for school assemblies, or Sunday clubs? We wrote a script for 'Lost!' and it worked really well. Everyone enjoyed it, especially the gang! You don't have to dress up much. We wrote our own scripts from the story and then read from them, so didn't have to learn lines. Props can be imaginary. We put actions to the narrators' bits and created our own sound effects. Here's how it went:

Narr. 1: Meet the Clubhouse gang! Their Clubhouse is a treehouse, built in the garden of: PAUL. He's rich, good-looking (!), clever and successful in everything he does. Yeah! Then there's Samantha—sorry! SAM. She's tomboyish, funny, sporty. A real good friend! Here comes NATHAN. He's scruffy, misunderstood, he gets things wrong even when he gets things right! But you can't help liking him! Then last, but not least, there's JESSIE. She's colourful, bright, fun and (shhh!) she goes to church—but she's OK! Except that today she's ill *(J holds stomach, as though sick)*, so she's off school. *(Raises hands in celebration then quickly goes back to looking ill again.)* Our story begins at the school gate. Nathan (who's pretty miserable today) and Sam (who's doing her best to cheer him up) are joined by Paul.

Sam: Hiya! Good job someone's cheerful today!

Paul: That's 'cos the Clubhouse is finally finished. We've got a place of our own, at last! Come and see it after school. It's brilliant! *(Nathan stuffs hands in pockets and walks away.)* What's up with him?

Sam: His mum's lost her job, his gran's lost her teeth, and his sister refuses to lose herself! Oh, yes, and his dad's working abroad again, so it'll be six months before he sees him.

Paul:	That's a bit rough. *(Catches Nathan up.)* Hey, I know what'll cheer you up! Come with me at lunch-time and help me feed my cockroaches!
Narr. 1:	YUK!!
Nathan:	Definitely YUK!
Narr. 1:	But Paul doesn't think they're yuk—he thinks they're brilliant! He's watched each one of them hatch out of their individual eggs, and now has seven different species. He brought them into school last week, and they're in a special tank in the lab. He's got tiny cockroaches and huge cockroaches! *(Paul holds hands very wide apart)* Not that huge! He's got brown ones, speckled ones, black ones, flying ones...
Paul:	They're one of the oldest types of winged insects in the world, dating back 350 million years!
Narr. 1:	AND he's got names for all twenty-five of them!
Paul:	Shh! Don't tell them I've given them names! They think I'm daft just liking cockroaches!
Narr. 1:	No one will ever know! On their way into school, Paul is stopped by Miss Grant, their form teacher.
Miss Grant:	Ah, Paul, you offered to help in the library this week. I'd like you to do that at lunch break, please. The weather is dreadful, so I doubt anyone's going to get outside today.
Paul:	*(with resignation)* Yes, Miss Grant.
Narr. 1:	After lunch Paul goes to the lab *(Paul lifts the lid off the imaginary tank)*, deciding his cockroaches need him more than the library does! He's just counting them, which he does every day, and letting some of them crawl up his sleeve *(sounds of general disgust from cast)*,

	which he also does every day, when Miss Grant comes in.
Miss Grant:	Paul, you're supposed to be in the library. You can't have forgotten, surely?
Narr. 1:	Well, Paul would rather stay with his cockroaches but, a promise is a promise, so he hurriedly shakes the insects off his arm, taking one last look at them, and follows the teacher out of the lab.

Narr. 2:	2,000 years earlier, on a sun-baked hillside overlooking Nazareth in Israel, JOSHUA *(enter Joshua, looking old)*, is looking after his one hundred sheep. *(Bleating sounds from cast.)* He knows there's a hundred, because he counts them every day, and can recognize every single one of them. His wife doesn't believe that, though. *(Miriam enters.)*
Miriam:	You can't possibly tell one from another, Joshua! A sheep is a sheep, is a sheep!
Joshua:	*(to audience)* She's wrong, you know. I've seen these sheep being born—tiny spindly little things they were, too. I know each one as if they're my own children. In fact, they're my friends! Why, I've even *(stage whisper)* got names for each of them!
Narr. 2:	*(to Joshua)* Names for each of them? You haven't!
Joshua:	Don't tell my wife. She thinks I'm daft enough as it is!
Narr. 2:	She'll never know! *(Narrator smiles foolishly as Miriam exits past!)* On this particular day, Joshua has just finished counting his sheep

	when Hanani, his friend, clambers up the hill, calling for him.
Hanani:	*(looking exhausted from the climb)* Hey, Joshua, you promised to help me mend my walls today. You've forgotten, I can see.
Joshua:	*(grimacing)* No, I was just about to remember! But my sheep...
Hanani:	My son, Kenaz, will be pleased to look after them. *(Enter Kenaz looking anything BUT pleased!)*
Narr. 2:	Joshua would actually rather stay with his sheep! But, a promise is a promise, so, taking one last look at his flock, he follows Hanani down the hill. *(Kenaz herds imaginary sheep off the stage. More bleating from cast.)*

Narr. 1:	Paul is worried! He's back in the lab after school, with Nathan this time, and has counted the cockroaches again, but can find only twenty-four!
Paul:	Nathan! Count these cockroaches for me.
Nathan:	What?! *(horrified!)*
Paul:	I think one's missing. Count them and see what you make it.
Narr. 1:	Nathan really doesn't want to but, very bravely *(Nathan flexes muscles!)*, helps count anyway.
Nathan:	Definitely only twenty-four. *(Starts looking around his feet, worried.)*
Paul:	Rats! It must've still been on my sleeve when I closed the tank up at lunch-time. *(Drops to his knees.)* Help me find him!

Narr. 1:	*(to Paul)* Him?
Paul:	Mad Max. 'Cos he charges around like a mad thing!
Nathan:	Why do we have to find it?
Paul:	Because he might get trodden on, or get too cold, or not find enough to eat, and die. I like my cockroaches—it's important!
Narr. 1:	Paul couldn't bear the thought of losing any one of his insects, so they went off in different directions and looked, and looked, and looked, until it was beginning to get dark, wet and windy *(sound effects)* and Nathan's stomach decided it was time to go home for tea! *(Rumbling sounds!)*
Paul:	*(joining him)* You sound like a gorilla in pain! Here, have a chocolate bar.
Nathan:	Cor, thanks! *(Nathan exits.)*
Narr. 1:	Paul kept on looking for a while longer, without success, eventually giving up, making his way home through the heavy rain *(sound effects)*, slipping on a damp piece of grass *(sound effect as Paul falls)* and grazing his shin *(loud 'ouch' from cast)*. He sat, drenched through, and found himself muttering something approaching a prayer:
Paul:	If you're there, God, help me find Max tomorrow, huh? Jessie says you're always listening, so maybe you could prove it! Minor miracle stuff. How about it?!

Narr. 2:	The wall had taken a long time to fix. When Joshua got back to his flock it was very hot, and

	Kenaz was asleep under a tree. *(Snoring from cast.)*
Joshua:	Hey! *(Prods him.)* Wake up.
Kenaz:	*(jumping up)* Sorry! I didn't mean to fall asleep. The sheep are fine. Look!
Joshua:	We must count them. You will help me.
Kenaz:	Count them! Why?
Joshua:	In case any are missing.
Narr. 2:	So they counted, and one was missing, so Joshua said:
Joshua:	We must look for her.
Narr. 2:	*(to Joshua)* Her?
Joshua:	*(to Narrator)* Eve. The firstborn.
Kenaz:	Why do we have to bother—you've got ninety-nine others!
Joshua:	Because she might get hurt. There are lions *(pointing at the audience as though they are the predators!)*, leopards, bears, wolves, hyenas, jackals, snakes and scorpions out there.
Kenaz:	Yes, I can see!
Narr. 2:	Joshua couldn't bear to lose any one of his sheep, so they went off in different directions to look for her. They looked, and looked, and looked, but they couldn't find her. It was very hot, and tiring, and Kenaz finally decided it was time for lunch. He was getting very hungry! *(Rumbles!)*
Joshua:	*(joining him)* You'll frighten off the rest of my sheep with all that noise! Here, have some bread.
Kenaz:	Oh, thanks! *(Exits.)*

Narr. 2:	Joshua kept looking, getting hotter and more tired, until he slipped on a rock and scraped his shin. *('Ouch' from cast.)* Sitting in a heap on the ground he called out:
Joshua:	Lord, I know you're listening! How about a little help to find my sheep? That shouldn't be too difficult, since you already know where she is! Just a little miracle—huh?
Narr. 1:	Next day at the school gates, Paul is miserable. *(Sam and Nathan enter behind Paul.)*
Sam:	Hey, Paul, guess what's for lunch today? Cockroach soup! Tasty! Jessie's still off school, but I saw her last night, and she suggested you make a poster:
Jessie:	*(from side lines, holding up large poster)* 'LOST COCKROACH. WANTED FOR LOOKING DISGUSTING! CAPTURE DEAD OR ALIVE!'
Paul:	Ha, ha, very funny! Anyway, I think her illness is affecting her brain. She said last night:
J & P:	*(in unison)* You haven't lost a cockroach, Paul, you've lost a sheep, and Luke knows all about it.
Nathan:	*(to Paul)* Who's Luke?
Paul:	No idea. What I do know is we've got Combined Sciences this morning. Old Deakin's going to expect to see twenty-five cockroaches in the tank! He'll go spare when he sees one's missing.
Narr. 1:	*(Paul, Nathan and Sam go into 'class', sitting on chairs placed by cast members.)* Mr Deakin is bald, thin, severe, and doesn't much like

children! *(Enter Mr Deakin, peering at the audience with dislike)*

Mr Deakin: This morning we will study the intriguing world of insects! And no squirming from any of you! Wheel the tank over, Paul. *(Paul is gazing intently at Mr Deakin's feet.)* Bridges!

Paul: *(jumping)* What?

Mr Deakin: Bring the tank over. Now!

Paul: Now? Er—yes! *(Stands, suddenly clutching his stomach, groans, and collapses near Mr Deakin's feet.)*

Mr Deakin: What on earth are you doing? Get up at once!

Nathan: *(kneeling down beside Paul)* What's the matter?

Paul: My cockroach! It's on Deakin's right shoe—it'll be climbing up his trouser leg next!

Nathan: He's been ill all week, Mr Deakin. It's this bug that's going round.

Sam: *(suddenly seeing the cockroach)* That's right! A really nasty BIG bug!

Narr. 1: Then Paul has a terrible coughing fit, lurching forward across the teacher's foot (which Mr Deakin doesn't like one bit), and retrieves Mad Max.

Mr Deakin: Pull yourself together, Bridges. Get the tank at once!

Narr. 1: Paul, grinning from ear to ear, carries the lost cockroach in his hand over to the tank.

Paul: *(putting the cockroach back in the tank)* My lost cockroach, safe and sound. A miracle, or what!

Narr. 2:	Joshua slept on the hillside with his flock, woke with the dawn and began to search again. This time he heard Eve bleating *(one person bleats)* and, crawling to the edge of the cliff *(use climbing frame, edge of stage, etc. for change of height)*, sees that she's standing on a ledge against a thin but sturdy tree—the only thing stopping her toppling into the valley far below. He knows he needs help—fast! *(Joshua starts to run.)* Stop! He's an old man! Not that fast! *(Joshua hobbles to side.)*
Joshua:	*(cupping hands to mouth)* Hanani, Kenaz, I need rope and your help to rescue my sheep!
Kenaz:	*(running to join him, followed by Hanani)* Is she alive then?
Joshua:	Yes, but we must hurry.
Narr. 2:	They lower Kenaz down the cliff, managing to pull up the sheep, then bring Kenaz back to safety. Joshua, grinning from ear to ear, carries his precious sheep back to the rest of the flock.
Joshua:	My lost sheep, safe and sound. Now that's what I call a miracle!

Narr. 1:	Jessie is now well, and, inside their Clubhouse, the gang is celebrating... *(Enter gang, with chairs, to form semi-circle.)*
Paul:	Crisps!
Sam:	Fizzy lemonade!
Jessie:	Chocolate bars!
Nathan:	More chocolate bars!

Narr. 1:	... the safe return of Paul's cockroach! (Any excuse for a party!) Hey, hang on a minute, though, Jessie. What was all that about the cockroach really being a sheep, and Luke knowing all about it?
Paul:	Oh, I figured that out. You can tell I'm the brains of the outfit! Found it in the school library Bible. Luke 15, verses 1 to 7. It's a story about a shepherd who loses one of his hundred sheep, and spends ages searching for it, then celebrates with all his friends when he finally finds it.
Sam:	Just as daft as you, really!
Paul:	I'll tell you what, though, that story must've been about my cockroach, too—not just about a dirty great sheep!
Jessie:	Oh yeah, how do you figure that one out?
Paul:	Well, I found another version of that story in Matthew, and that says, 'God doesn't want any of these little ones to be lost.' Sheep aren't little. My cockroach is, though!
Sam:	Isn't! It's huge!
Jessie:	Doesn't mean either—it's a parable.
Nathan:	What's a parable?
Jessie:	A story that explains one thing by talking about another. Jesus meant that, like the shepherd, God really cares about every single one of us—no matter who we are.
Sam:	Just like Paul and his adorable cockroaches, really!
Paul:	Sounds fair enough to me! *(Stands, with can in hand.)* A toast! To a day which has been, without question, the best one of my entire life... so far!

GROUP REMAINS IN PLACE, MAKING A STILL TABLEAU THROUGHOUT FINAL SECTION

Narr. 2: Later that day, Joshua is sitting around a fire with friends and family, celebrating...

(Group enter with bench or similar, joined by Mr Deakin and Miss Grant, now as Joshua's friends.)

Hanani: Wine!

Kenaz: Barley loaves!

Miriam: Fish!

Joshua: More wine!

Narr. 2: ... the safe return of his sheep.

Miriam: Though why we have to have a party just because that sheep hadn't the sense to stay with the rest of the flock in the first place, I really don't know...!

All: *(to Miriam)* Shh!

Joshua: *(raising his drinking cup)* Drink a toast with me, my friends! For this has been, without question, the best day of my entire life!

THIS GROUP ALSO HOLDS A STILL TABLEAU FOR A FEW SECONDS.

Also from BRF

If you've enjoyed reading Clubhouse Stories, look out for Who, Me? Paul, a fast-moving, action-packed account of the great apostle's amazing adventures.

Paul was a great saint; a small man with a big voice. He didn't start out as a saint. He hated the very idea of Jesus, and had his followers arrested. Then one day God spoke to Paul. 'I have chosen you to serve me! Go, spread my name throughout the world!' Paul never did anything by halves. With laughter and song he endured shipwrecks and beatings, was stoned, arrested, and escaped from Damascus in a basket. He travelled thousands of miles on foot, but everywhere he went he told people about Jesus. A terrible worrier, when he couldn't talk to people direct he wrote powerful letters to encourage and guide new Christians. Nearly two thousand years after he died, Paul's voice still echoes round the world.

Relevant Bible passages, background information and illustrations are interwoven into the story, which closely follows the events recorded in the Acts of the Apostles and includes some of Paul's 'famous' passages.

£3.99 ISBN 1 84101 021 9
Available from your local bookshop or direct from BRF (£3.99 plus £1.25 postage and packing).